Deutschland im Spiegel seiner Filme

CiLT
Centre for Information
on Language Teaching and Research

The Centre for Information on Language Teaching and Research provides a complete range of services for language professionals in every stage and sector of education, and in business, in support of its brief to promote Britain's foreign language capability.

CILT is a registered charity, supported by Central Government grants. CILT is based in Covent Garden, London, and its services are delivered through a national collaborative network of regional Comenius Centres in England, the National Comenius Centre of Wales, Scottish CILT and Northern Ireland CILT.

CILT Publications are available through all good booksellers or directly from:

Grantham Book Services Ltd
Isaac Newton Way
Alma Park Industrial Estate
Grantham, Lincs NG31 8SD
Telephone: 01476 541 080
Fax: 01476 541 061

Deutschland im Spiegel seiner Filme

Edited by Martin Brady and Helen Hughes

Modern German Studies vol. 1
Series Editors: Jim Jordan and Gisela Shaw

First published 2000 for AMGS
by the Centre for Information on Language Teaching and Research (CILT)
20 Bedfordbury
London
WC2N 4LB

ISBN 1 874016 98 4

Printed in Great Britain by Copyprint (UK) Ltd.

CILT Publications are available from: Grantham Book Services, Isaac Newton Way, Alma Park Industrial Estate, Grantham, Lincs, NG31 8SD. Tel. 01476 541080. Fax: 01476 541061. Book trade representation (UK and Ireland): Broadcast Book Services, 2nd Floor, 248 Lavender Hill, London, SW11 1JL. Tel: 020 7924 5615. Fax: 020 7924 2165.

Contents

Foreword

This is the first in a new series of volumes to be published by the Association of Modern German Studies. The series has been created to collect and publish selected papers presented at one-day conferences organised by the Association. It aims at all those interested in the German-speaking countries, but in particular at those who teach the German language and related studies in secondary and higher education. It is intended to complement the Association's already established practise of producing *Arbeitsmaterialien* – materials for debate and suggested use in the classroom – accompanying its one-day conferences.

The Association was founded in 1982 in collaboration with the Goethe Institut London. Its object, expressed in its constitution is 'to provide a forum for all teachers and other persons interested in the society and culture of the German-speaking countries, to bridge the gap between institutions where German is taught at a secondary and tertiary level and to promote co-operation with organisations representing the German-speaking countries'. The editors hope that the series will be a contribution towards that aim.

We are grateful to the following collegues who gave valuable editorial assistance in the preparation of this volume in advance of the series having a permanent editorial board: Dr Philip Brady, Birkbeck College, London, Dr Robert Burns, University of Warwick, Professor Peter

Lutzeier, University of Surrey, Dr Margaret Rogers, University of Surrey, Professor John Sandford, University of Reading.

The creation of this series owes much to the work of Sue Myles, lecturer in German at the University of Middlesex, who sadly died before this first volume could be completed. Our early editorial meetings were much assisted by her forthright and humorous presence as series editor. It is intended to dedicate the second volume of this series on *Migrants in German-speaking countries: aspects of social and cultural experience* to her memory.

This volume on German film is dedicated to Dr Philip Brady, a founder member of the Association, who also died before the production of this volume. His help was much valued and is much missed.

1 | Introduction: Films and texts

Helen Hughes
University of Surrey

1 Films and conferences

In recent years there has been a rapid increase in the availability of German films on video and via satellite television. As a result many teachers of German are using film as a valuable resource for courses on society, history and literature, as well as in language teaching. There are, of course, an enormous range of possible ways of incorporating film – be they fictional or documentary – into German Studies. They all differ fundamentally, however, from the methods of studying film within Media and Film Studies which tackle films as objects of study in and of themselves.[1] The aim of the three one-day conferences on German cinema organised by the Association for Modern German Studies during 1995 and 1996 was to respond to the increasing demand for practical material on the use of films in teaching German. The title of the second and third of these events, and the one chosen for this publication, *Deutschland im Spiegel seiner Filme*, programmatically places the

---

1 The approaches I am referring to here are formal or film historical, dealing with the aesthetics of filmmaking and its stylistic development. Useful introductory works on the theories underpinning stylistic movements and on the relationship between technical developments and international film styles are to be found in Andrew (1984), Bordwell and Thompson (1990), Thompson and Bordwell (1993). Hickethier (1993) provides an excellent systematic introduction in German to the language of filmmaking in all its aspects. The film dictionary *Film Talk* (Bartsch and Read, 1993), arranged into three main sections, '*Vorbereitung*', '*Produktion*' and '*Nachbereitung*', is useful for the development of vocabulary (pointing out in the introduction that English is the primary language for film production today), although it is, of course, rather technical.

emphasis fairly and squarely on the ways in which films can be used to introduce students to various aspects of German life.

The first of the conferences, '*Literaturverfilmungen*', tied in with an international conference held at the Goethe-Institut in 1993 on 'Film and Literature in the New German Cinema', also organised by the editors of this volume, and examined what remains the mainstay of German cinema in the classroom – adaptations of classic or contemporary literary texts. The second, '*Deutschland im Spiegel seiner Filme: Themen und Unterrichtsmethoden*', moved away from issues relating to adaptation to consider the ways in which films may be used to stimulate language-learning and debate about German society and culture in the context of Area Studies and topic teaching. Themes addressed included old standards such as *Vergangenheitsbewältigung, Ausländer-feindlichkeit* and the Third Reich, together with the issue of gender and the history of the GDR. Finally, '*Deutschland im Spiegel seiner Filme II: Heimat, Identität und Ideologie*' moved the discussion on to the specific question of how film has reflected on the national and regional identity of German culture, its sense of place, of people, of history, and how films continue to reflect on contemporary society in Germany and its increasing diversity within a European context.

Discussion at all of these events involved issues of methodology . How can film be used productively at different levels of secondary and higher education? When is it appropriate (or feasible) to show an entire film? How can extracts be selected and incorporated into language classes? How can film clips be combined with text-based activities? How reliable are feature films as social or historical documents? How can we contextualise films for students and take advantage of their status as records of social and political change? Whilst the *Arbeitsmaterialien* provided by the speakers for the conferences addressed practical questions such as availability of material, and presented specimens of classroom activities, the papers in this volume are intended to introduce a range of methodologies for approaching films both as documents and cultural products and making best use of them to explore the major issues confronting post-war Germany.

Unfortunately, not all the presentations given at the conferences could be reproduced in this volume. Many were designed as workshops and represented work-in-progress and/or approaches to stimulating class discussion. This means that important themes have been left out – the role of film in the GDR, [2] for example, and the role of women in German film.[3] Material relating to these discussions has, however, been presented in the Association's *Arbeitsmaterialien*. The papers selected for this volume thus do not claim to represent the whole debate; rather, they are representative in the way they cover a diverse range of topics whilst at the same time displaying considerable diversity in their approaches to the material.

2 Films and literature

Literaturverfilmungen remain the favourite 'set texts' in schools and universities.[4] Often regarded either as a painless introduction to literary classics and linguistically challenging contemporary literature, or as a means of introducing other media to the curriculum without sacrificing the literary canon entirely, literary screen adaptations or films by *Autorenfilmer* (writer-directors) understandably dominate the classroom. Ostensibly literary adaptations offer the best of both worlds – a safe bridge linking the cultural heritage to the new media. Whilst this can undoubtedly be the case under ideal circumstances, experience has shown that the result can often be an unhappy mix of trivialised literature and turgid cinema. And, what is more, a film judged purely by the standards of the book it adapts rarely passes muster. The thorny question of whether, and if so how, an adaptation can do justice both

2 Film in the GDR has, for obvious reasons, been a major topic of debate during the last few years. Fortunately two major volumes have been published providing comprehensive information on the production and development of film during the 40 years of the state's existence. Schenk (1994) deals with the production of feature films in the GDR, whilst Jordan and Schenk (1996) covers the history of GDR documentary. Allan and Sandford (1999) contains studies of individual films and genres in the GDR.

3 Here I am referring both to women as filmmakers and to the representation of women in German filmmaking. Neither of these topics was covered as such during the one-day conferences, but they too have been major issues recently. Julia Knight (1992) points out the increasing prominence of women directors in German filmmaking during the 1980s. The two volumes of *Gender and German Cinema* (Frieden et al, 1993) provide a series of papers addressing themes relating to film and the representation and emancipation of women.

4 Bauschinger (1984), Rentschler (1986) and Paech (1988) all testify to the importance of literary adaptation as an object of study and comment on its importance within the history of German filmmaking.

5

to film and the literary source is addressed by Martin Swales in his analysis of Fassbinder's *Fontane Effi Briest*, and Martin Brady in his comparison of two adaptations of Kleist's *Novelle, Die Marquise von O... .* Martin Swales points out that Fassbinder is able in his adaptation to reflect critically on the character of the nineteenth-century realist novel in the very process of transfer into the medium of film. The twentieth-century reader, well versed in the conventions of the realist novel, is made aware, through techniques derived from Brechtian theatre, of both the distance and the proximity of Fontane's society and times. In comparing two films which claim absolute fidelity to to their source material, Martin Brady points out that even here the adaptation of the literary text is essentially a starting point for the filmmaker's own vision, rather than an end in itself.

3 Films and society

Certain literary adaptations have gained almost canonical status not because of the authors of the source material, but because of the themes they address. Obvious examples would be Schlöndorff and von Trotta's *Die verlorene Ehre der Katharina Blum* and Schlöndorff's *Die Blechtrommel.* This brings us to a second application of film in the classroom – as a social and political document, as a window or mirror on German society past and present. [5] The nature of this mirror and the extent of its potential distortion is addressed by Guido Rings in his examination of one of the most popular *Autorenfilme* of the New German Cinema – Fassbinder's *Angst essen Seele auf,* the story of a middle-aged German cleaning woman who, to the dismay of her family and friends, marries a Moroccan immigrant worker. In an approach which draws on the methodology of Area Studies, Guido Rings shows how Fassbinder's 'politicised weepy' engenders an empathetic understanding of the position of so-called *Gastarbeiter* in the Germany of the Economic Miracle. At the same time he supplements the film's fictional narrative with revealing statistical information relating to the history of resentment amongst the German population towards mass immigration. This exemplary comparison between the social scientist's

---

5 Studies of the New German Cinema in particular have looked at the attitudes of a whole generation of *Filmautoren* towards the past and present of German society: (Sandford, 1980, Rentschler, 1984, Elsaesser, 1989, Kaes, 1989).

data and the society as represented in a work of screen fiction demonstrates how factual information may reflect positively or negatively on the film's own didactic intentions. If positive, the film can be presented in the classroom as a contribution to a deeper, more sympathetic understanding of a theme such as racism; if negative, however, the data collected by the social scientist may point out the ways in which the film reiterates destructive impulses within a particular society, becoming a contribution in itself to prejudice or misunderstanding.

This approach to teaching film, using it within a *Landeskunde* or topic-orientated context, naturally selects out films which reflect explicitly on social and political issues, thereby drawing on a different canon from that represented by literary adaptation. Fassbinder's *Angst essen Seele auf* is perhaps the most obvious example, but the approach demonstrated by Guido Rings could be applied to films as diverse as Fritz Lang's *Metropolis* (technology and the city), Brecht's *Kuhle Wampe* (unemployment, the Weimar Republic and the rise of Hitler), Wolfgang Staudte's *Rotation,* Konrad Wolf's *Ich war neunzehn* and Helma Sanders-Brahms's *Deutschland bleiche Mutter* (the Third Reich, *Vergangenheitsbewältigung* in East and West), Wenders's *Im Lauf der Zeit – Kings of the Road* (the fatherless post-war generation), the collective film *Deutschland im Herbst* (terrorism), Reinhard Hauff's *Der Mann auf der Mauer* (German division), to the more recent films such as Heiner Carow's *Coming Out* (homosexuality and the GDR) and von Trotta's *Das Versprechen* (the *Wende*). These films, chosen pretty much at random, reflect on changing attitudes in German society across a wide range of themes: the workings of capitalism, the nature of cities, its ways of coping with the division of Germany, its treatment of outsiders, its respect or disrespect for its laws and democratic institutions, its attitudes towards sexuality.

4 Films and audiences

Up to this point the articles have tended not only to focus on films of the last few decades (the period of the so-called New German Cinema), but also on canonical 'arthouse pictures'. Whilst placing socially critical

7

films in their historical context tells us a good deal about filmmakers' attitudes and the society they work in, it has been felt increasingly in recent years that many of the films chosen for such analyses tend not to have made any great impact in Germany itself and to have been seen by relatively small audiences. As we know, audiences generally prefer to be entertained rather than educated in the cinema. For this reason many cultural historians have argued that the selection of films for study and analysis should be widened to include more representative, popular films seen by truly mass audiences. Such a shift in the object of analysis would necessarily bring with it a different kind of approach, one taking into account not only the context of the film's production, but also the history of its reception.

What is at stake here is not an extension of the canon, or 'dumbing-down' by pandering to popular culture, but a new kind of historiography. Some progress was made in this direction to coincide with the centennial celebrations in 1995, and in the classroom Cultural Studies methodologies have carried on this work. The first comprehensive survey of the entire history of German film, *Die Geschichte des deutschen Films* (Jacobsen et al, 1993, pp.7–12.), summarises the many ways in which film history can be written: in the context of social and political history, in a national or an international context, as part of the history of art, as the history of film production, as a succession of genres, as a roll-call of great inventors, directors, cinematographers or actors, or as a chronology of film titles and movements. At the same time it is stressed that the films themselves ultimately evade historical categorisation, continually being reinvented in different contexts from that of their creation, and decoded anew by successive audiences. This revealing process of reception is the subject of articles on the cinema of the Third Reich by Erica Carter and Alasdair King in this volume. [6]

Questions of spectatorship and reception, the role of popular culture in an academic context and the general issue of what kind of film is

---

6 Two other periods which have been revisited in the spirit of extending the study of German film into popular entertainment are the periods before Weimar Expressionism and the 1950s, both often written off by film histories for their lack of 'serious' films. Studies providing information on the films of these periods include Schlüpmann (1990) and Berger (1989).

chosen for teaching and research, are addressed in Erica Carter's 'What is German cinema? Approaches to popular film'. Her article identifies and defends a significant shift away from the study of German film as art, as an inventory of classics, towards an analysis of popular cinema and box-office hits. Again, the change requires a new set of skills drawing, for example, on oral history, Intercultural and Gender Studies, psychoanalysis and Media Studies. As Marc Silbermann puts it in *German cinema: Texts in context* (1995, p.x), what matters are 'the intersections of various practices: theory and analysis, interpretation and empiricism, text and context.' What is learnt is that a 'film's meaning is produced in a context, and every film is historical in the way it positions the spectator in relation to this context through characters, narrated events, atmosphere, facts, and fictions.' (p.x)

In his article on Veit Harlan's enormously successful melodrama *Die goldene Stadt*, seen by an audience of over 30 million, Alasdair King draws on Area Studies and Cultural Studies methodologies to present an exemplary analysis of a popular film produced during the Third Reich. In his exploration of spectatorship, ideology and the representation of national identities he demonstrates the insights that can be gained for teaching and research by shifting the focus to popular culture.

5 Films and mirrors

The final paper, 'Narcissism and Alienation: Mirror-images in the New German Cinema' by Andrew Webber, also addresses the controversial question of the construction of a national identity in Germany. In its title and focus on four classic films of the New German Cinema (Fassbinder's *Effi Briest*, Wenders's *Im Lauf der Zeit*, von Trotta's *Bleierne Zeit* and Reitz's *Heimat*) it also takes us back full circle. Addressing both the title and subtitle of the third conference ('*Deutschland im Spiegel seiner Filme: Heimat, Identität und Ideologie*'), Andrew Webber adopts a psychoanalytical approach to what might be termed the cinematic deconstruction of German post-war identity in the New German Cinema.[7] In examining the question of how film can be a national

---

7 For an introduction to psychoanalytic approaches to film interpretation, in particular the theories developed by Lacan, see Stam (1992), pp.123–142.

mirror – albeit at best a fragmented or distorted one – his paper not only ties in with those of Erica Carter and Alasdair King, but also returns us to the issue of how and why films can be used to reflect on Germany itself.

This collection of papers is presented in the order in which they were delivered at the conferences in London and York. It is a sequence which, we believe, demonstrates many revealing ways in which films have been introduced and utilised in teaching and research in German Studies. We hope that the volume as a whole will be seen as a contribution to the meaningful integration of German film into the discipline.

Bibliography

Allan S and J Sandford, *DEFA: East German Cinema, 1946–1992* (New York, Oxford, Berghahn, 1999)

Andrew D, *Concepts in film theory* (Oxford, Oxford University Press, 1984)

Bartsch A and P K Read, *Film talk* (Hamburg, Verlag für Medienliteratur, 1993)

Bauschinger S et al, *Film und Literatur: Literarische Texte und der neue deutsche Film* (Berne, Munich, Francke, 1984)

Berger J et al (eds), *Zwischen Gestern und Morgen – Westdeutscher Nachkriegsfilm 1946–1962* (Frankfurt am Main, Deutsches Filmmuseum, 1989)

Bordwell D and K Thompson, *Film art: An introduction* (New York etc, McGraw-Hill, 1990)

Corrigan T, *New German Cinema: The displaced image* (Bloomington, Indianapolis, Indiana University Press, 1994)

Eisner L H, *Die dämonische Leinwand* (Frankfurt am Main, Kommunales Kino, 1975)

Elsaesser T, *The New German Cinema: A history* (Houndmills, London, BFI Macmillan, 1989)

Frieden S et al, *Gender and German cinema: Feminist interventions. Volume I: Gender and representation in New German Cinema. Volume II: German film history/German history on film* (Providence, Oxford, Berg, 1993)

Hickethier K, *Film- und Fernsehanalyse* (Stuttgart, Weimar, Metzler, 1993)

Huillet D and J-M Straub, 'Gespräch mit Danièle Huillet und Jean-Marie Straub' in: Schütte W (ed) *Klassenverhältnisse: Von Danièle Huillet und Jean-Marie Straub nach dem Amerika-Roman 'Der Verschollene' von Franz Kafka* (Frankfurt am Main, Fischer, pp.37–58, 1984)

Jacobsen W et al (eds), *Geschichte des deutschen Films* (Stuttgart, Weimar, Metzler, 1993)

Jordan G and R Schenk (eds), *Schwarzweiß und Farbe: DEFA-Dokumentarfilme 1946–92* (Berlin, Jovis, 1996)

Kaes A, *From Hitler to Heimat: The return of history as film* (Cambridge Massachusetts, London, Harvard University Press, 1989)

Kluge A (ed), *Bestandsaufnahme: Utopie Film: Zwanzig Jahre neuer deutscher Film / Mitte 1983* (Frankfurt am Main, Zweitausendeins, 1983)

Knight J, *Women and the New German Cinema* (London, Verso, 1992)

Kracauer S, *From Caligari to Hitler: A psychological history of the German film* (Princeton, Princeton University Press, 1947)

Kramer T (ed), *Reclams Lexikon des deutschen Films* (Stuttgart, Reclam, 1995)

McCormick R, *Politics of the self: feminism and the postmodern in West German literature and film* (Princeton, Princeton University Press, 1991)

Paech J, *Literatur und Film* (Stuttgart, Metzler, 1988)

Pflaum, H G and Prinzler H H, *Film in der Bundesrepublik Deutschland* (Bonn, Inter Nationes, 1992)

———. *Cinema in the Federal Republic of Germany* (Bonn, Inter Nationes, 1993), a translation of *Film in der Bundesrepublik Deutschland* (Bonn, Inter Nationes, 1992)

Phillips K (ed), *New West German filmmakers: From Oberhausen through the 1970s* (New York, Frederick Ungar, 1984)

Rentschler E, *West German Film in the course of time* (Bedford Hills, New York, Redgrave, 1984)

———. (ed), *German film and literature: Adaptations and transformations* (New York, London, Methuen, 1986)

———. *The ministry of illusion: Nazi cinema and its afterlife* (Cambridge, Mass., Harvard University Press, 1996)

Ruttmann W, 'Kunst und Kino', in: Goergen, J (ed) (n.d.) *Walter Ruttmann: Eine Dokumentation* (Berlin, Freunde der Deutschen Kinemathek pp.73–74, c.1913)

Sandford J, *The New German Cinema* (London, Oswald Wolff, 1980)

Schenk R (ed), *Das zweite Leben der Filmstadt Babelsberg: DEFA-Spielfilme 1946–1992* (Berlin, Henschel, 1994)

Schlüpmann H, *Unheimlichkeit des Blicks: Das Drama des frühen deutschen Kinos* (Basel, Frankfurt am Main, Stroemfeld/Roter Stern, 1990)

Silberman M, *German cinema: Texts in context* (Detroit, Wayne State University Press, 1995)

Stam R, *New vocabularies in film semiotics: Structuralism, post-structuralism and beyond* (London and New York, Routledge, 1992)

Thompson K and D Bordwell, *Film history: An introduction* (New York etc, McGraw-Hill, 1993)

Welch D, *Propaganda and the German cinema 1933–1945* (Oxford, Clarendon, 1983)

Witte K, 'Wie Filmgeschichte schreiben?' in: *Film und Fernsehen in Forschung und Lehre* (Nr 5, 1982)

2 | Fassbinder's *Fontane Effi Briest*: An exercise in interrogative intertextuality

Martin Swales
University College, London

Rainer Werner Fassbinder was an extraordinarily – indeed, overtly – mannered film director. Even when his theme, as was the case with *Katzelmacher* or *Angst essen Seele auf*, was a critique of narrow-mindedness in contemporary German society, he elected to argue not through straightforward (that is, relatively un-self-conscious) realism but through insistently foregrounded stylisations of image, soundtrack, and dialogue. For a director who made such remarkably few concessions to what one assumes to be the prevailing taste of the mass cinema-going public, it is intriguing to wonder how he came to command the very considerable public following that he enjoyed. [8] (In this context it may be pertinent to recall that the two golden ages of German cinema – the Weimar years, and the period from roughly the late 1960's to the mid 1980's – were dominated by, if the crude distinction may be allowed, 'artistic' rather than straightforwardly narrative cinema; in other words, Fassbinder did not have to fight for the right to be stylistically self-conscious, in the way that a Peter Greenaway or a Derek Jarman have to do battle with their native film tradition.)

Yet mannerism and emphatic stylisation are not in themselves virtues; and on occasion Fassbinder's art can seem a monumental triumph of style over substance (I think, in this context, of *Die bitteren Tränen der*

---

8 John Sandford speaks of 'the sheer volume of Fassbinder's production and the relative popularity of his appeal'. (1980, p.64)

14

Petra von Kant). But *Fontane Effi Briest* is, in my view, a towering masterpiece because it legitimately foregrounds issues of style and mode. Fassbinder offers us the scrupulous filmic statement of a preexisting literary work – Theodor Fontane's novel of 1895. In a way that may, I suspect, be well-nigh unique within *Literaturverfilmungen*, Fassbinder makes us perceive the novel genre itself through the film; Fontane's text is not just some tentatively acknowledged source, not a mere story-line, nor is it the basis for some filmically transformed screenplay, as is the case with Luchino Visconti's *Death in Venice.* Rather, the mode and manner of the late nineteenth-century novel are insistently present in the narrative argument of the film. Fassbinder simply does not allow the gap between his late twentieth-century filmgoers and the late nineteenth-century novel text to close – because that gap is cognitively important, both for him and for us. That is to say: at one level, we are made to respect and enter late nineteenth-century narrative conventions; at another level we are made to notice – because of its obtrusiveness and strangeness – the ways in which the novelistic style asserts itself at the expense of filmic flow. Hence the mannerism of which I spoke. But it is a mannerism that seeks to betray (in both senses of the word, to bear the imprint of and to call into question the belief in) the stylistic and thematic particularities of the late nineteenth-century novel and of the world from which it derives and to which it refers. Fassbinder's film is an extended act of historical and aesthetic quotation. In a way that would, I suspect, have given enormous pleasure to Bertolt Brecht, it constantly makes us perceive the characters' experience as formed both by the society of which they are part and by the literary modes of representation that are of a piece with that society's self-understanding. Fassbinder's mannerism here is not self-regarding or wilful; rather, it is central to an act of artistic and socio-historical questioning, to a creative project of truly thoughtful intertextuality.

Fassbinder was, of course, anything but unknowing about the kind of film which he had made. It is not for nothing that the title of the film invokes not just the name of the heroine but also – and in first place – the name of her literary maker: *Fontane Effi Briest.* Fassbinder on one occasion (1986, p.54) observed that the upshot was …

> *... ein Film über Fontane. [...] Es ist ein Film, der eine Haltung nachvollzieht. Es ist die Haltung von einem, der die Fehler und Schwächen seiner Gesellschaft durchschaut und sie auch kritisiert, aber dennoch diese Gesellschaft als die für ihn gültige anerkennt.*

In other words, the literary mode was uppermost in his mind. In the interview from which I have just quoted, he reports significant disagreements with Hanna Schygulla who wanted to play the role of Effi much more as the dramatic story of an oppressed woman of the late nineteenth-century (Fassbinder, 1986, p.59). Fassbinder was adamant; the film was about a novel before it was a film about a woman.

Indeed, so strenuously intertextual is the governing artistic will that the end product is, initially at any rate, somewhat forbidding. When I first saw it shortly after it came out on general release, it had the effect of largely emptying the cinema in which I was sitting. The cinema was situated in no lesser a university town than Cambridge, and many of those who left before the end were students. All of which tallies with Fassbinder's admission (1986, p.56) that he was writing ' *für Leute, von denen ich einen bestimmten Bewußtseinsgrad denke voraussetzen zu können*'. But I do not think one can blame those students for getting fidgety, because the Fassbinder film really is held on a very tight rein. The moments of genuine, unmediated emotion are few and far between (if they exist at all). The film shows us dignified, touching, but ultimately entrapped creatures, entrapped not just by the ' *Gesellschafts-Etwas*' which Fontane explores so superbly, but also by the omnipresence of the literary, cultural, and linguistic medium in which they live, move and have such being as they can muster; and that medium is the late nineteenth-century realistic novel of family life, of adultery, of letters discovered and duels fought, of the family as source of comfort and protection and as the nexus of conflicting norms and aspirations. Fassbinder invites us to notice and be critical of that convention; but he is careful not to break with it, nor to displace it. Rather, he respects it at every turn while constantly putting it in quotation marks.

I want now to comment briefly on the various devices by which the film holds its experiential statement at one remove – almost behind glass, as it were. Let me begin with the words, with the text we hear (and on

16

occasion see). Fontane, as is well known, is a master of conversation. Fassbinder follows him in eavesdropping on the various social occasions at which the characters interact. There is an unmistakable air of the heavily quotational about such scenes in the film. Apart from the three main characters, whose words were all spoken by the performers in question (Hanna Schygulla as Effi, Wolfgang Schenk as Innstetten, and Karlheinz Böhm as Wüllersdorf), the soundtrack for all the other figures was provided by actors and actresses other than those we see on the screen. There is, in other words, something of speech-at-one-remove to the film's soundtrack. The characters are spoken rather than speaking; they go through the discourse and the motions of their lives. And something of this even applies to the principal actors. Karlheinz Böhm is dignified and predictable as are all those figures in the Sissy and other films that he made in his youth. Hanna Schygulla is, of course, as pretty as a picture – indeed, at frequent intervals throughout the film she appears as in a picture frame. Her voice is high-pitched, doll-like and curiously inexpressive. Take what ought, on any calibration of the emotional thermometer, to be her great moment – the outburst of despair after the disastrous interview with Anni who destroys her mother with the relentless repetition of the modal verb of decent upbringing – '*oh gewiß, wenn ich darf*'. Effi pours out her rage and despair at the transformation of a child into a marionette. Schygulla speaks the monologue hunched over a chair; we only see her face from the side, in part framed by the ornamental carving of that chair. The anguish is affecting, touching; but the immovable position of the actress and the invariability in terms of pitch, colouring, and pace of her delivery makes the whole scene statuesque rather than lacerating. Once again, Fassbinder knew exactly what he was doing; he refers at one point to the '*Verfremdung*' achieved '*durch das emotionale Spiel der Schauspieler*' (1986, p.61). Or perhaps more accurately he should have said '*das nicht-emotionale Spiel der Schauspieler*'.

On frequent occasions Fassbinder ensures that the characters' utterances are literally at one remove; that is, he uses a narrative voice-off on the soundtrack which reports what the characters say or think – and the voice we hear is none other than Fassbinder's own. This means that their inwardness is constantly quoted rather than coming to us as a form of direct disclosure. This is the case with such key moments as Effi's fear when she is left alone in the house in Kessin, as her self-interrogation about her lack of guilt-feelings in respect of the adultery with Crampas. The voice-off tells us that she lays her head on her arms and weeps; but we see no such thing. The image before us throughout this monologue is of an elegant young woman walking under an umbrella through the rain. Much of the verbal seduction of Effi by Crampas is entrusted to the voice-off – as is her mother's repudiation of her, and her final speech about shooting stars and the heaven above her. Fassbinder never allows us to forget the narrative texture of the nineteenth-century novel. Moreover, there is a degree of neutrality to the way that the narrating voice speaks. There is no attempt at drama, at public appeals to us for sympathy and understanding. Nor is the voice withheld such that it sounds like our private reading to ourselves. Rather, it is as though the novel were being read aloud; the reciting voice is held at some middle ground, a constatation of the historical presence of the classic literary text. (The contrast could hardly be greater with John Huston's film *The dead* which derives from the last story of James Joyce's *Dubliners.* Huston's film is a delicate and wistful tribute to a fragile world that, because of the emotional temperature of the Christmas and New Year period which constitutes its temporal setting, is acutely aware of its own transience. Huston has the breathtaking final paragraph of Joyce's tale spoken by a voice-off. The voice-off, like the words it speaks, is gentle. But there is an immense urgency to its plea that we acknowledge our own mortality. Huston's immediacy is poles apart from Fassbinder's reserve.)

The final point which should be made about the verbal material of Fassbinder's film is that much of it is made visual by means of what one can best liken to Brechtian *Spruchbänder.* They consist of phrases taken from the novel text which are projected as sayings, as proverbial utterances – and the actual typographical format is the old German script, the '*Fraktur*' of the nineteenth-century novel text. Some of the phrases which are thus highlighted are manifestly of central interpretative import (e.g. the '*Angstapparat aus Kalkül*', e.g. '*ich kann von vielem in meinem Leben sagen "beinahe"*'). The latter phrase speaks of the all-pervasive sense of inauthenticity which is the governing signature of those extensively socialised lives which both Fontane and Fassbinder put before us. Most importantly: we actually see the father's telegram to his daughter – '*Effi komm*'. As in Fontane's novel, the echo of the early scene where Effi is summoned from the meeting with her future husband to 'come and play' with her three girlfriends is both powerful and telling. The father's moment of emotional spontaneity and need in defiance of all social caveats is undercut by the reminiscence that tells us that he was also complicit in the upbringing of his daughter which left her so unprepared for the adult role which she was expected to play. The visual image of the telegram, then, is an interpretatively weighty statement because it suggests that the parents make both their daughter and the social destiny that destroys her. However, other moments of visually displayed text are nowhere near so momentous. One thinks, for example, of ' *es war stille im Hause*'. The effect in this case is simply to sustain the level of discursive, readerly statement in the film. We are constantly reminded of that narrative that in every sense discursively contextualises and constructs the life it puts before us. And in that aesthetic contextualisation we perceive the social conditioning operative in the experiences we witness. The issue of conditioning is raised in the very opening frame which, somewhat in the manner of an eighteenth-century novel, provides a sententious subtitle to the work we are about to see. That subtitle reads:

> *Viele, die eine Ahnung haben von ihren Möglichkeiten und ihren Bedürfnissen und trotzdem das herrschende System in ihrem Kopf akzeptieren durch ihre Taten und es somit festigen und durchaus bestätigen.*

This matter of the text made visible brings me to the whole question of the visual statement, of the camera placement that informs the entirety of the film.

The first aspect to register is that the film is made in black and white with frequently a soft focus that reminds one of old photographs. Fassbinder was careful to use precisely the kind of film that recalls the visual impact of silent films; the relatively slow film speed means that there are half tones between black and white. Moreover, the technical limitations of the film necessitated artificial lighting not only for interior scenes – but also for external shots (Iden et al., 1985, pp.172–3). Hence the somewhat stagey quality to so many of Fassbinder's images. Groups look as though they have been posed for the camera – whether they consist of outside scenes (Effi and her playmates, the picnics with Crampas), or of interiors (Effi receiving visitors in Kessin, the Innstetten/Wüllersdorf discussions.) On the whole, the camera remains at a middle distance, whereby the individual is always elaborately framed and set in context. There are few close-ups in the film: the chief ones are Innstetten's face at the '*Effi komm*' moment, the close-up of the mother when Herr von Briest wonders if Innstetten would not have made a better husband for her, the close-up of Effi listening to the Spohr song, of Effi writing to her mother announcing her pregnancy, and of her face, framed by the chair, in the monologue of despair after the meeting with Anni. But on the whole, such moments are as rare as are the moments of intense private inwardness in Fontane's novels. What prevails is, as it were, the proscenium arch of nineteenth-century bourgeois drama. The fourth wall is taken away to reveal neither the private recesses of the soul nor mass scenes and grandiose historical panoramas, but rather the space occupied and inhabited by the bourgeois and minor aristocratic family. One constantly has the sense of passing from one family occasion to the next. Fassbinder is fond of the white-out to mark a transition in the action. Scenes end in total whiteness. And they start in that whiteness with the camera lens then narrowing down to find the right exposure. Fassbinder (1986, p.55) comments on this technique as follows:

> *Schwarzblenden sind ja meistens Gefühls- oder Zeitblenden. Weißblenden sind dagegen Wachmacher, denn allein durch das Weiß, das denn da ist, erschrickt man ein bißchen, kriegt einen kleinen Schock und bleibt wach, [...] wach im Verstand.*

The appeal to our critical intelligence has, of course, to do with the foregrounded literariness of the film. The constant intrusion of whiteness reminds one of turning the pages of a book as we move from one chapter to the next. Moreover, the white-out serves to underscore the materiality of the medium which confronts us – it is light passing through celluloid. It is perhaps also worth mentioning (albeit in an age of ubiquitous video-watching) that, as a further contribution to Brechtian *Verfremdung*, the white-out in the cinema constantly obliges us to register ourselves, the audience, as onlookers at a film.

By far the most striking feature of the visual statement in Fassbinder's film is the immense fondness for framing and replicating devices. Constantly the camera perceives a character or a group of characters through an aperture – a doorway, a window, an arch. Never can they break free of the containing mould which they carry round with them. Not even when they are outdoors do we sense that they are released from the containing, regimenting structure of their lives. Walks in the countryside have a recurrent sameness to them – often they approximate to a march in Indian file (one thinks of Effi's walks with her mother, and, on a visit to Hohen-Cremmen from Kessin, with her father). This self-replicating quality is central to Fassbinder's purpose. On two occasions the camera accompanies Effi on a walk through the rain; the duel is fought on the beach that forms the setting for the picnics. Nothing in the film is unique, is inalienably particular or individual. Time and time again the characters' experience consists of replicas. This issue finds explicit enactment in the insistent use made of mirrors. The characters constantly find themselves surrounded by their own elaborately framed image. In one of the absolutely supreme sequences of the film Fassbinder situates the crucial discussion between Innstetten and Wüllersdorf about the duel in a proliferation of mirror images. Both in Fontane and Fassbinder the key issue is that of 'Verschwiegenheit' – of whether or not there can be such a thing as secrecy. In both cases, more is at stake than the extent of Wüllersdorf's reliability and tact. Rather, it emerges that Innstetten cannot believe in secrecy because he carries the public realm round with him, because he is society to his own selfhood. At this crucial moment Fassbinder films both participants to the conversation as located in an elaborate nexus of mirrorings. At one point, Innstetten is framed in the central section of the mirror, but out of focus, whereas Wüllersdorf is a double image at the edge, in focus, surrounding Innstetten.

The whole handling of this conversation is nothing short of virtuosic. And it is the one section in the film where Fassbinder departs from the sequential narrative and scenic chronology of the late nineteenth-century novel mode. As Innstetten and Wüllersdorf move agonizingly round the question of the duel and the offence which it is meant to expunge, we frequently cut from the two men talking to shots of a train in motion – and subsequently to a horse-drawn carriage. The suggestion is clear: as the two figures debate and agonise, the implication is that metaphorically the journey has already started; the decision has already been taken, as Gaby Schachtschabel (1984, p.172) observes. In an anachronistic world where horse-drawn carriages coexist with railway trains, the anachronism of the duel is still very much alive. And the issue of anachronism, of asynchronicity, of ' *Verjährung*' is at the centre of Innstetten and Wüllersdorf's discussion of the duel. [9] But all the anguishedly civilised argument leads only to the brutality of the pistol shot. In a violent cut, which comes as a great shock in a film in which, as I have already observed, so many scenes end with a slow white-out, the pistol is fired instantly at the end of the discussion between Innstetten and Wüllersdorf. No sooner is the decision made than we find ourselves at the site of the duel in Kessin – on the beach that we have seen so often before. All the uncertainty and soul-searching has been mere prevarication; the outcome, like so much that these characters know and say and do, is a foregone conclusion.

Mention of that brutal pistol shot brings me to the soundtrack. I have already mentioned the insistent presence of the narrative voice-off. But there are sounds which seem initially to lift us clear of the endless discourse of socialised experience. There are two kinds of auditory signal for such intimations of seeming freedom. One is, in the scenes set in the countryside, the presence of bird song and dogs barking. I think, for example, of the moment when Effi meets Roswitha at the cemetery. The noises-off are unnaturally loud – almost as though they were quotations from an instantly recognizable tape of countryside background noises, available to any film or radio producer, rather than being the real thing. Even the birds in Fassbinder are quoted – sung rather than singing. The other dominant feature of the soundtrack, and it recurs in so many of the interior scenes, is music. There is not just the repeated violin phrase by Saint-Saëns, one thinks also of the various pieces of music that are performed by the characters – the Spohr song sung by Tripelli, Wüllersdorf's fondness for the Beethoven piano sonatas. The salient point in all these cases is that the music does not manage to break the hold of socialised and socializing discourse. The

---

9 I am very grateful to my colleague and friend William Larrett for a particularly thoughtful and detailed discussion of this scene.

violin phrase is a sweet accompaniment to heartache, but no more than that. Not even the glorious slow movement of the Beethoven *'Pathétique'* sonata, which Wüllersdorf delights in playing, creates a realm alternative to that of societal discourse; rather, it wistfully accompanies and reinforces it. Often we find that the piano is not simply – perhaps not essentially – a musical instrument. It is primarily a splendid piece of furniture in the aristocratic household. And, given the high gloss which adorns its surface, it too is another of those containing and replicating mirrors to which I have already drawn attention.

Let me draw to a close and offer some concluding thoughts on Fassbinder's achievement in his *Fontane Effi Briest* film. I want to begin at the end by concentrating on the closing image of the film. Fassbinder is, as so often, scrupulously faithful to his original; and the final scene consists of the discussion between husband and wife as to whether they might not have been in some way responsible for the catastrophe. Herr von Briest calls a halt to all such speculations with a version of one of his favourite conversational ploys – *'das ist ein zu weites Feld'*. As is the case with the novel, so here too in the film, characters part perceive and part fail to perceive the motivation and causality at work in their own lives. The dialogue comes to rest in a gesture of resignation, of not pressing the point. And Fassbinder then holds the final shot for what seems to be an eternity. The camera tracks back slightly but keeps in frame husband and wife, the breakfast table, the trees, the swing, and the house. The father continues smoking, a leaf falls, he drinks from his coffee cup, and the sound of the cup being replaced on the saucer is unnaturally vivid (given our distance from the group) on the soundtrack. In a way that seems to me utterly in tune with Fontane's purposes, the final image is one of the simple, unremarkable continuity of family and social life. Coffee is served, unemphatic conversations recur, and the experiences that are beyond the pale are kept precisely beyond the pale – and out of shot. Of course, events have occurred that are remarkable, distressing, incommensurable; they have made inroads into and taken their toll of these framed lives. But ultimately the frame remains intact, and the camera acknowledges and respects that frame that both entraps and sustains those characters.

23

The last shot of the film of course reminds us of the first one. For the eponymous heroine of both novel and film, Hohen-Cremmen is both the alpha and omega of her life. The novel and the film show us Effi on the swing at these key moments. Fassbinder is, in my view, truer to Fontane than many scholarly commentators in that he sees Effi on the swing not as some ethereal spirit, not as a ' *Naturkind* or dryad, nor even as an anarchical tomboy, but essentially as the high-spirited product of her parents' upbringing and training. When she gets off the swing, not a hair is out of place. She is as ready (or unready) as she ever will be to meet her intended, to outstrip her mother in social rank. The first image we have in the film is of the wonderfully pretty, doll-like Hanna Schygulla; it comes as no surprise when this Effi says about the man she will marry: ' *Jeder ist der Richtige. Natürlich muß er gut aussehen und eine Stellung haben.*' The issue of social conditioning is crucially present in the child's upbringing. We will be reminded of the opening scene many chapters later in the disastrous interview between mother and daughter. Effi, looking at Anni, describes her as ' *wild und ausgelassen beim Spielen*', and adds '... *hast du von deiner Mama.*' But that, we feel, is as little true of Anni as it was of Effi – and no doubt, of her mother before her who recognises in Effi's so-called tempestuousness a reminder of her own youth. All three women are drilled, regimented creatures who believe they have or have had moments of spontaneity and untrammelled high spirits. But that belief does them precious little good. Ultimately the regimentation carries the day – both in the social world of which they are part and in the aesthetic mode which articulates their story.

One final point: for a variety of reasons we as contemporary readers can, I suspect, find relatively immediate access to Fontane's novel whereas Fassbinder's film strikes us as highly mannered. We are, after all, still very close in our novelistic assumptions and expectations to the conventions of nineteenth-century realistic fiction, and Fontane is the most engaging of story-tellers – with the result that we are allowed an unproblematic entry into the world of his fictions. No great demands are made on the reader's suspension of disbelief, no sudden, grandiose symbolic intimations are thrown at us. For page upon page we seem simply to eavesdrop now on one group of characters, now on another. The patterns and symbols are, of course, there; but they are in the nature of unemphatic hints, the '*Finessen*' of which Fontane was so proud – rather than heavily asserted, clamorously meaningful stylisations.[10] By contrast with Fontane's understatement, the Fassbinder film does seem very portentous, very knowing; we simply cannot overlook the strenuously aesthetic manner of the telling. There is nothing in a filmic sense casual about Fassbinder's narrative. Rather, as I have already suggested, the conventions of the nineteenth-century realistic novel are foregrounded and made strange by being transposed onto film. Perhaps, in the process, the characters and their experiences are drained somewhat of their immediate humanity. They are museum pieces rather than vulnerable creatures, whereas Fontane's world seems to speak much more directly to us despite the hundred-year gap between it and our contemporary world. Fontane's characters do not feel as programmed, conditioned, regimented as do Fassbinder's. The latter are like insects trapped in some elaborate housing. Fassbinder resists all temptation to assimilate the story of Effi Briest to late twentieth-century filmic expectations; he neither modulates into slick, fast-moving realism nor into post-modernist delight in the self-conscious play of signs, symbols, artistic modes in their irremediable contingency. Instead, he both draws attention to and also leaves intact the artistic modality of Fontane's narrative. He makes us notice (rather than take for granted) what the novel narratives of classic realism are – and he asks us to perceive their all-pervasive character. In consequence, we recognise that realism in the Fontane mode – however immediate and natural it may seem to us – is never a natural (that is unmediated) replication of a world out there. Realism is a convention, it is part of the agreements and conventions, both literary and extra-literary, of its age; it depends upon '*Pakt und Übereinkommen*' (Fontane, 1960, p.185). In ways that remind us powerfully of Brecht, Fassbinder invites us both to criticise the conventions and to perceive their operative power in the lives before us, to recognise that both the signs and the lives can and should be changed – but that there are no (as it were post-modernist) wands that will accomplish it overnight.

---

10 I would maintain this even in spite of Karl Guthke's (1982) celebrated onslaught which accuses Fontane of being overt to the point of pretentiousness. Guthke, in my view, fails to distinguish between those moments when the characters wittingly seek to express and on occasion magnify their self-understanding through symbolic statement and the novelistic sub-text which intimates symbolic connections to which the characters are largely impervious.

When Fassbinder looks back to Fontane's Wilhelmine world he perceives – to borrow a favourite phrase of Raymond Williams's – a whole 'structure of feeling' that informs both social life and its fictional modes. Hence the insistently interrogative intertextuality of his filmic debate with his predecessor. The intelligence and critical perception are quite magnificent. The foregrounded aesthetic manner is at one with the critical enterprise; and it is, I suspect, a critical enterprise that Fontane would have recognised, and, up to a point at any rate, welcomed. And if that is true, then it makes Fassbinder's film a truly remarkable exercise in *Literaturverfilmung* understood as that process of intertextual creativity whereby the two media are constantly, insistently present, and interrogate each other across the historical, referential, and discursive gap that separates them.

26

Bibliography

Fassbinder R W, 'Bilder, die der Zuschauer mit seiner eigenen Phantasie füllen kann: Ein Gespräch mit Kraft Wetzel über *Fontane Effi Briest*' in: *Fassbinder, Rainer Werner,* edited by M Töteberg, *Die Anarchie der Phantasie* (Frankfurt am Main, Fischer, 1986)

Fontane T, edited by H-H Reuter, *Schriften zur Literatur* (Berlin, 1960)

Guthke K S, Fontanes '*Finessen*' – '*Kunst*' oder '*Künstlerei*'? *JDSG*, vol. 26, pp.235–26, (1982)

Iden P et al, *Rainer Werner Fassbinder.* Reihe Film 2. (Munich, Hanser, 1985)

Sandford J, *The New German Cinema* (London, Wolff, 1980)

Schachtschabel G, *Der Ambivalenzcharakter der Literaturverfilmung, mit einer Beispielanalyse von Theodor Fontanes Roman 'Effi Briest' und dessen Verfilmung von Rainer Werner Fassbinder* (Frankfurt am Main, Bern, New York, Nancy, Lang, 1984)

3 | 'Mann kann bei einem Autor kein Wort verändern.' The Marquise von O... adaptations of Eric Rohmer and Hans Jürgen Syberberg

Martin Brady
King's College, London

1 Literary adaptation

From the outset German cinema has been inextricably bound up with literature and literary culture. The most conspicuous manifestation of this is a superabundance of *Literaturverfilmungen* For his book *German film and literature: Adaptations and transformations* Eric Rentschler compiled a substantial list of literary adaptations, which, moreover, lays no claim to completeness. His chronological survey records 120 literary adaptations between 1913 and 1932, 109 between 1933 and 1945 and a staggering 549 between 1945 and 1985, including 152 produced in the GDR. In all, Rentschler's list comprises 778 feature-length *Literaturverfilmungen* (Rentschler, pp.336–365) Furthermore, any catalogue of the most famous or influential German films would be likely to include a good number of literary adaptations: Murnau's *Tartüff*, Pabst's *Die Büchse der Pandora*, von Sternberg's *Der blaue Engel*, Harlan's *Opfergang*, Staudte's *Der Untertan*, Straub/Huillet's *Nicht versöhnt*, Wenders's *Angst des Tormanns beim Elfmeter*, Schlöndorff's *Die Blechtrommel*, Herzog's *Woyzeck*, Fassbinder's *Berlin Alexanderplatz* to name but a few. There are indeed many major German directors, including Murnau, Harlan, Schlöndorff and Straub/Huillet, who have rarely strayed beyond literary adaptation. [11]

---

[11] It has also been argued that all films based on screenplays are de facto literary adaptations. In the present context, however, the focus is on the adaptation of independent works of literature. Thomas Elsaesser (1989, p.108) indeed argues that it is 'quite wrong to speak of literary adaptation as a genre' given the broad range of popular and art films that come into this category.

Despite the unmistakable success of filmed literature, Volker Schlöndorff for one has felt it necessary to put up a vigorous defence of his commitment to literary adaptation:

> *An author usually spends years working on a book, and even when he's not actually writing, then he is constructing it inside himself ... . When you're writing a film script you take perhaps eight weeks – all right, let's say three months –: the result can't be the same. I'm not trying to rule filmscripts out of court, I'm just saying that I prefer to film literature because I don't know anyone here who could dedicate himself in quite the same way to a film script – I know I certainly couldn't.*[12]

This position is not, however, without its detractors. Filmmakers and critics alike have accused Schlöndorff and other confirmed *Literaturverfilmer* of the New German Cinema such as Hans W. Geissendörfer of laziness, a paucity of imagination or of subjugating film to the tyranny of the literary heritage. Yet the positions for and against literary adaptation are far from clear cut: for example, even such stridently individual voices as Fassbinder and Herzog have, as the films listed above testify, turned to literature for inspiration. Literary adaptation touches on issues as diverse and controversial as cultural legitimation and national identity, film subsidy (for example the relative ease during the seventies of attracting funding to a project based on a literary classic), and intellectual freebooting.

The debate is also not exclusive to the New German Cinema and the so-called '*Literaturverfilmungsdebatte*' of the seventies. In a spirited letter to a friend in 1917, the experimental and documentary filmmaker Walter Ruttmann (n.d., p.73) derided colleagues for their cowardly dependence on literature, declaring '*Literatur hat aber mit dem Kino nichts zu tun!*'. A decade later the Dadaist filmmaker Hans Richter (1981, p.43) summed up his standpoint, and that of fellow avant-gardists with the assertion that '*Film von Natur aus weder mit dem Roman noch mit Theaterstück [sic] Nennenswertes gemein [hat]*'More recently, in his stock-taking of the successes and failures of the New German Cinema,

---

12   Quoted in Sandford (1981, p.151).

Bestandsaufnahme: Utopie Film, Alexander Kluge (1983, p.436) asserted with his usual forthrightness that literary adaptations are *sui generis* doomed to failure:

> *Die Filmgeschichte scheint zu beweisen, daß die Literatur-verfilmungen immer ärmer sind als die Literatur. An den bloßen Resultaten: 'es sind zwei verschiedene Medien und deshalb liegt ihre Fähigkeit, Reichtum an Ausdruck zu produzieren, auf verschiedenen Gebieten', läßt sich der Ausweg nicht ablesen.*

2 Literary cinema

It is with Kluge, however, that we come to an important distinction which allows some common ground to be pinpointed between those undertaking literary adaptation and those arguing for the emancipation of film as film. In his remarks Kluge does not intend to imply that German cinema is not itself 'literary'. As John Sandford has rightly observed, 'wordy' is a term commonly used to characterise the films of the New German Cinema, those of Kluge foremost amongst them. Its essentially verbal nature has tended, he notes ...

> *... to confirm still further the popular foreign image of the New German Cinema as 'earnest' and 'cerebral' – not only because of its concentration on literary texts, but because German literature, from which most of the texts are taken, has in any case a long tradition of emphasizing the ratiocinative at the expense of the sensuous!* (p.152)

Thomas Elsaesser points out that the discursive quality of the New German Cinema derives from the conviction on the part of the *Autorenfilmer* that filmmakers have the 'right to self-expression and [...] demand to use film as the medium for a personal vision' (p.43). The film *auteur*, they argue, has the same status as the literary author, an argument which implies that his or her voice is essentially a literary one. In the founding manifesto of the German New Wave, the 1962 *Oberhausener Manifest*, the term *Autorenfilm* is used as a rallying call and an approximate equivalent of the French *cinéma des auteurs,* the films of the French New Wave on which the young German directors of the sixties modelled themselves so avidly. As Annette Brauerhoch (1991, p.155) has put it in an essay entitled *Der Autorenfilm: Emanzipatorisches Konzept oder autoritäres Modell*

> *Am Autorenfilm wird also vor allem die Kunstwürdigkeit des Films diskutiert, erst der Filmautor hebt den Film aus namenloser Unterhaltung und kommerzieller Industrie. Der Film wird, literarisiert, der Betrachtung erst wert. Der Name des Autors überstrahlt die Mitwirkung anderer am Film, er wird seinerseits zum zirkulierenden Warenwert und fokussiert die Filmwahrnehmung auf eine der Literatur ähnliche hin, nämlich auf das Filmwerk.*

There is clearly a potential for conflict here in the context of literary adaptation. It is conceivable that an *Autorenfilmer* could lose his or her distinctive (literary) voice in speaking through the words of another. Whilst it has frequently, and at times rightly been argued in the case of certain adaptations that such a loss has occurred, it is my contention that the *Marquise von O...* films of Rohmer and Syberberg demonstrate that even a slavish adherance to the literary source material need not imply – at least in the hands of an outspoken *auteur* – a loss of voice.

3 Adaptation and fidelity

Returning to the issue of the adaptation of literary texts, as opposed to the question of the literary film, the problem of focussing on the verbal at the expense of the visual is not one restricted to the filmmakers themselves. It is also a predicament that affects the viewing experience and critical discourse about film. The prevailing trend of the *Literaturverfilmung* debate has been to assess a given film's fidelity to the text on which it is based. This 'discourse of fidelity', as it has become known, tends to take a literary text as a starting point and applaud a filmmaker for reverence to the original author's perceived intentions. The filmmaker is often expected merely to illustrate the text visually and is castigated if he or she deviates from this role.

Perceived or expected fidelity to the text has also in the past tended to

31

be a primary motivation for including literary adaptations in the curriculum both in secondary and higher education. The fact that films introduced into the classroom to illustrate set texts are invariably a disappointment and a source of confusion for students (why is so much of the text missing? ... did he really say that? ... where is so-and-so?) is proof that a *Literaturverfilmung* cannot re-present a literary work accurately on screen. What is more, very few set out to do so. Indeed there would be little point in doing so given the fundamental differences between page and screen highlighted by Kluge in the passage quoted above. A distinctive and successful literary adaptation will invariably reveal more about the filmmaker and the age in which he or she lives than about the text chosen as source material.

The film historian Christopher Orr (1984, p.72) summarises the problem neatly as follows:

> *The concern with the fidelity of the adapted film in letter and spirit to its literary source has unquestionably dominated the discourse on adaptation.*

> *Given the problematic nature of the discourse of fidelity, one is tempted to call for a moratorium on adaptation studies. On the other hand, the literary source does affect the production and consumption of the film adaptation and we run the risk of impoverished film studies by ignoring this fact.*

However, with the rapid growth in recent years of Film Studies as a discipline in its own right, the emphasis has naturally shifted from the text to the film: to investigate what a given film is saying **with** a text, **about** a text, **through** a text, **with the help of** a text or, even, **against** a text (and indeed its author). This shift in emphasis within the discourse on film has perhaps taken its lead from the filmmakers themselves. For example, since the early 1960s the most radical of *Literaturverfilmer,* Jean-Marie Straub and Danièle Huillet, have adapted Böll, Bruckner, Corneille, Brecht, Mallarmé, Pavese, Duras, Kafka, Hölderlin, Sophocles and others in the belief that a literary text affords unique insights into the historical, social and political make-up of a nation and its people, at the time both of its genesis and its reception, and that a *Literaturverfilmung* must always regard the text as a starting point, not an end in itself:

> *Man muß zuerst wissen, was einen interessiert oder nicht. Das wissen die meisten Leute in unserer Welt schon gar nicht mehr. Und man muß wissen, was mit den eigenen Erfahrungen zu tun hat, d.h. was einen trifft oder nicht. Denn man 'verfilmt' ja nicht ein Buch, sondern man setzt sich mit einem Buch auseinander, man will einen Film aus einem Buch machen, weil das Buch mit eigenen Erfahrungen zu tun hat, mit eigenen Fragen, eigenen Haßausbrüchen oder mit eigenen Liebeserklärungen. Als erstes fange ich dann an, abzuschreiben.* (Schütte, 1984, p.46)

4 The two Heinrichs

One of the manifest conclusions to be drawn from Rentschler's extensive survey of literary adaptations is that, despite the vast range of possible source material, there is a clear tendency among filmmakers in West Germany to cluster around a small number of tried and trusted authors. A number of authors have fallen prey to this tendency, most conspicuously the two Heinrichs – Böll and von Kleist. By 1980 there had been no fewer than nineteen Böll adaptations produced by directors as diverse as Herbert Vesely, Jean-Marie Straub and Danièle Huillet, Uwe Brandner, Volker Schlöndorff and Margarethe von Trotta, and Vojtech Jasny. This phenomenon was examined by a number of speakers, including the present author, at the symposium 'Heinrich Böll on page and screen', organised jointly by the Goethe Institut London, Institute of Germanic Studies and Birkbeck College in December 1995. [13] In what follows I wish to focus on the case of Heinrich von Kleist. The idea of comparing the two *Marquise von O...* adaptations was proposed in discussion by Hans Jürgen Syberberg, who suggested that it would be revealing to compare and contrast his version of the story with that of the French director Eric Rohmer, which he himself admired greatly. Such a comparison is a revealing exercise, not least because the same actress, Edith Clever, plays the protagonist in both films, Rohmer's of

---

[13] The proceedings of this conference have been published in the *University of Dayton Review* vol. 24, no. 3 (1997).

1976 and Syberberg's of 1989. Given the unavailability of Syberberg's film and its relative unsuitability for teaching – at nearly four hours it is extremely long and has yet to receive serious critical attention – the emphasis in what follows will be on Rohmer's version, which has been readily available on video in Britain for a number of years.

It is not my intention here to present even a limited interpretation of these two films, but merely to demonstrate that scrupulous adherence to the letter of the text is no bond of fidelity.

5 Kleist and film

Before turning to the films themselves it is helpful to consider what it is that has attracted so many filmmakers to Kleist. Syberberg himself, for example, has made four Kleist adaptations – *San Domingo* (1970), *Penthesilea* (1987), *Die Marquise von O...* (1979), and *Ein Traum, was sonst?* (1995) which uses substantial passages from *Prinz Friedrich von Homburg*. There are also Kleist films by, amongst others, Volker Schlöndorff (*Michael Kohlhaas*, 1969), George Moorse (*Der Findling*, 1967), Helma Sanders-Brahms (*Das Erdbeben in Chili* in 1975 and the biographical portrait *Heinrich* in 1977) and Hans Neuenfels (*Heinrich Penthesilea von Kleist – Träumereien über eine Inszenierung* 1983). Furthermore, Kleist is not the sole property of the Federal Republic. Looking further afield one could also cite Gustav Ucicky and Emil Jannings's *Der zerbrochene Krug* of 1937 and examples from the GDR including Günter Reisch's *Jungfer, sie gefällt mir* of 1969, also based on *Der zerbrochene Krug*.

What has attracted so many filmmakers to Kleist, whom Elsaesser (p.87) terms 'the patron saint of the New German Cinema'? Elsaesser himself cites the themes of war and revolution in the *Novellen*, the double suicide and 'metaphysics of private revolt' (p.88) as important factors. The writer's proverbial 'modernity' has undoubtedly also played a major part in it, not least his forthright portrayal of physical and sexual violence (pivotally in *Die Marquise von O...*), his singular even-handedness in the portrayal of the sexes, and his fondness for caricaturing a pervasive modern disorder, hypocrisy. These qualities in particular help to illuminate the choices of Volker Schlöndorff and Helma Sanders-Brahms. It is, however, Kleist's prose style – so often nonchalantly referred to as 'cinematic' – which has, perhaps more than anything else, attracted filmmakers to his *Novellen* and plays.

6 *Das Erdbeben in Chili*

To demonstrate this I wish to turn briefly to the story chosen by Helma Sanders-Brahms, *Das Erdbeben in Chili*, in order to highlight a number of stylistic characteristics of Kleist's prose which may have attracted filmmakers.

(1) In St. Jago, der Hauptstadt des Königreichs Chili, stand gerade in dem Augenblicke der großen Erderschütterung vom Jahre 1647, bei welcher viele tausend Menschen ihren Untergang fanden, ein junger, auf ein Verbrechen angeklagter Spanier, namens Jeronimo Rugera, an einem Pfeiler des Gefängnisses, in welches man ihn eingesperrt hatte, und wollte sich erhenken. (Kleist, 1810, p.164)

What is striking about this opening sentence of the story is the literary 'zoom technique'. From the geographical and historical wide angle (a particular city in a particular year) we zoom in spatially and temporally to a close-up on an instant in the mind of a single man standing next to a pillar in a prison cell. The precision and economy of this zoom, which finds space to inform us of the outcome of the catastrophe, has the control of a tightly edited pre-credit sequence in a Hollywood thriller.

In the style of a flashback this sequence is picked up again, two pages later, where it was left off:

(2) Eben stand er, wie schon gesagt, an einem Wandpfeiler, und befestigte den Strick, der ihn dieser jammervollen Welt entreißen sollte, an eine Eisenklammer, die an dem Gesimse derselben [sic] eingefügt war; als plötzlich der größte Teil der Stadt, mit einem Gekrache, als ob das Firmament einstürzte, versank, und alles, was Leben atmete, unter seinen Trümmern begrub. (pp.165–6)

Here the zoom is reversed, out from the hook – which in a grammatically surreal construction appears to be attached to the very world itself – to the panorama of the catastrophe outside, accompanied by an appropriate sound effect. It is an improbable stroke of luck, worthy of a good B-movie, which allows the hero to escape: two buildings facing one another fall simultaneously and meet in the middle, forming an arch. What is remarkable about the account of the protagonist's escape is the detail and precision of the description of these falling buildings:

(3) *Der Boden wankte unter seinen Füßen, alle Wände des Gefängnisses rissen, der ganze Bau neigte sich, nach der Straße zu einzustürzen, und nur der, seinem langsamen Fall begegnende, Fall des gegenüberliegenden Gebäudes verhinderte, durch eine zufällige Wölbung, die gänzliche Zubodenstreckung desselben.* (p.166)

In a remarkable symbiosis of the verbal and visual, of the event and its representation, the construction of the sentence describing the collapse of the prison parallels the formation of the resulting arch, coming to rest at the comma separating the two cave-ins – ' *und nur der, seinem langsamen **Fall begegnende, Fall*** [my emphasis].

As the protagonist escapes through the burning city, Kleist depicts his flight in the manner of a story-board for a breathtaking tracking shot: an accumulation of terse clauses which drives the text precipitously forward to the staccato beat of nine repetitions of the word *'hier'*:

(4) *Hier stürzte noch ein Haus zusammen, und jagte ihn, die Trümmer weit umherschleudernd, in eine Nebenstraße; hier leckte die Flamme schon, in Dampfwolken blitzend, aus allen Giebeln, und trieb ihn schreckenvoll in eine andere; hier wälzte sich, aus seinem Gestade gehoben, der Mapochofluß auf ihn heran, und riß ihn brüllend in eine dritte. Hier lag ein Haufen Erschlagener, hier ächzte noch eine Stimme unter dem Schutte, hier schrieen Leute von brennenden Dächern herab, hier kämpften Menschen und Tiere mit den Wellen, hier war ein mutiger Retter bemüht zu helfen; hier stand ein anderer, bleich wie der Tod, und streckte sprachlos zitternde Hände zum Himmel.* (p.166)

36

All of this fire and brimstone is abruptly interrupted by a passage of pseudo-romantic lyricism, which turns out in retrospect to have been a dangerous and misleading illusion of calm and tranquillity before the next catastrophe. Interludes of this kind have, of course, become a cliché in all kinds of action films.

(5) *Indessen war die schönste Nacht herabgestiegen, voll wundermilden Duftes, so silberglänzend und still, wie nur ein Dichter davon träumen mag.* (p.170)

When this catastrophe finally comes – presaged by ominous examples of Kleist's renowned ' *als ob*' constructions, including a characterisation of the false idyll as a haven of serenity ' ***als ob*** *es das Tal von Eden gewesen wäre*' (p.170, my emphasis) – the result is the death of the two protagonists and the accidental and brutal murder of an innocent child. To capture the savagery of the denouement, Kleist resorts to a violently vivid style worthy of Quentin Tarrantino or John Woo:

(6) *Don Fernando, dieser göttliche Held, stand jetzt, den Rücken an die Kirche gelehnt; in der Linken hielt er die Kinder, in der Rechten das Schwert. Mit jedem Hiebe wetterstrahlte er einen zu Boden; ein Löwe wehrt sich nicht besser. Sieben Bluthunde lagen tot vor ihm, der Fürst der satanischen Rotte selbst war verwundet. Doch Meister Pedrillo ruhte nicht eher, als bis er der Kinder eines bei den Beinen von seiner Brust gerissen, und, hochher im Krise geschwungen, an eines Kirchenpfeilers Ecke zerschmettert hatte. Hierauf ward es still, und alles entfernte sich. Don Fernando, als er seinen kleinen Juan vor sich liegen sah, mit aus dem Hirne vorquellendem Mark, hob, voll namenlosen Schmerzes, seine Augen gen Himmel.* (p.181)

7 Rohmer's *Die Marquise von O...*

According to the majority of critics, Rohmer succeeded admirably in rendering Kleist's essentially cinematic prose on screen:

Rohmer exactly captures the breathless gravity of Kleist's style: a classical serenity stirred by a fierce undertow of agitation [...]. (Milne 1976/77, p.54)

[...] a work of muted amusement and of constant visual delight [...]
every detail bespeaks a painstaking sense of composition and mood
[...]. (Gow, 1976, p.33)

Scene follows paragraph with such fidelity that to read von Kleist
afterward is to re-see the movie in every detail.(Michener, 1976, p.36).

Thanks to such mastery, viewers who don't have an opportunity to
read Kleist's extraordinary novella – which is not easily available in
English – won't even be able to imagine what they're missing.
(Rosenbaum, 1976, p.253)

The outspoken American critic Pauline Kael (quoted in Gerlach, 1980,
p.84) was indeed one of the few to attack the film. According to Kael,
Rohmer's version is over-studied and de-eroticised, treating Kleist's
'highly filmable' original as if it were 'an official nineteenth-century
stage classic, to be given a wooden, measured reading'. The result, she
concludes, is the transformation of *Die Marquise von O...* into an
'historical work re-created for educational television' (quoted in
Gerlach, 1980, p.84).

Rohmer (1979a, p.111), a classical philologist who learnt German as part
of his spadework for this adaptation, is one of the most eloquent
advocates of his own film, and has explained with great lucidity in his
'*Anmerkungen zur Inszenierung*' and elsewhere what attracted him to
Die Marquise von O... . First, he claims that his intention from the outset
was to stay as faithful as possible to Kleist's   *Novelle* in order to explore
not only the text and its author, but also the period in which it was
written:

Dem Kleistschen Text Wort für Wort zu folgen, war das leitende
Prinzip unserer Verfilmung. Am liebsten würden wir bei dieser
Arbeit an einem klassischen Text die vergangene Welt mit der
gleichen Detailtreue zeichnen wie wir es in unseren 'Moralischen
Erzählungen' hinsichtlich der Welt von heute versucht haben.
Zweifellos kann eine solche Wiederherstellung niemals absolut
getreu sein. Unser Versuch ist kein wissenschaftlicher. Aber vielleicht
ist es möglich, durch die filmische Übersetzung Sitten und

Empfindungen einer vergangenen Epoche besser zu erfassen. Ein Werk verjüngen heißt nach unserer Meinung nicht, es zu modernisieren, sondern es in seine Zeit zu stellen.[14]

I shall return to the question of fidelity below. Second, in keeping with the first point, he argues that an adaptation can revitalise an important text which may have become something of a monument:

Es ist durchaus denkbar, daß in bestimmten Fällen eine filmische Inszenierung das klassische Werk vom Firnis, mit dem das Alter es überzogen hat, befreien kann und ihm – gleichsam wie das Restaurieren von Gemälden in den Museen – seine echten Farben wiedergibt. (p.111)

Third, and perhaps most significant, is his assertion that he chose the text, not merely because he felt an empathy for Kleist's urbane social criticism and manifest sense of humour, but also because Kleist's style is quintessentially cinematic, with all the necessary ingredients for the filmmaker in place. *Die Marquise von O...* is, he asserts, a screenplay waiting to be realised ' *ohne Vermittlung einer sogenannten "Bearbeitung"* ' (p.111).

In the light of the foregoing analysis of the stylistic features of *Das Erdbeben in Chili* it is worth quoting Rohmer's remarks in full:

Die filmische Übersetzung gelingt hier gleichsam wie von selbst und ist nicht, wie so oft, ein Kampf gegen eine widerstrebende Materie.

Erstens, weil die Dialoge des künftigen Films schon vollständig ausgearbeitet sind in einer Form, die gänzlich untheatralisch ist, die, wie wir meinen, glatt 'über die Leinwand gehen' müßten; weil die Dialoge in direkter Rede stehen, oder, in indirekter Rede geschrieben, äußerst leicht umzusetzen sind.

Zweitens, weil sich der Erzähler jegliche Andeutung der inneren Vorgänge seiner Helden versagt. Alles ist von außen her beschrieben

---

14   A slightly different version of this text appeared in   *Filmkritik* no. 229 (1976) under the title *'Bemerkungen zur Inszenierung'*.

und mit der gleichen Ungerührtheit betrachtet wie durch das Objektiv einer Kamera. Die Beweggründe der Personen lassen sich nur durch die Beschreibung ihres Verhaltens hindurch erahnen. Der Film ist also hier der Erzählung gegenüber nicht im Nachteil, da sie ja gerade ihre Möglichkeit zur Introspektion an keiner Stelle wahrnimmt.

Drittens, weil Kleist uns mit äußerster Präzision, besser als der gewissenhafteste Drehbuchautor, über die Gewohnheiten, Bewegungen, Äußerungen seiner Helden Auskunft gibt. In jedem Augenblick wissen wir, ob eine Figur steht, sitzt oder auf den Knien liegt, ob sie ihren Partner umarmt oder ihm die Hand reicht,... ob sie ihn anschaut oder den Blick abwendet. Wäre jede Zeile des Textes mit einem Stich illustriert, könnte dieser nicht besser unsere Vorstellungskraft ansprechen. (p.111–12)

In interview Rohmer cites, as an example of his transposition of Kleist's cinematic prose onto the screen, the conspicuous use of intertitles in his film – what he terms 'inserts' – claiming that he added them to demonstrate that Kleist's prose not only pre-empts sound cinema with its taut dialogue, but also silent cinema with its intense gestures and attention to eloquent milieu and settings:

Die Inserts, ja, ja. Und ich hätte in diesem Film wie bei den 'Moralischen Erzählungen' einen Erzähler gebraucht und eine Stimme, wie man sagt in englisch, im off. Aber ich wollte das nicht. Ich zog vor, die Zwischentitel zu schreiben. Für mich enthält Kleists Werk schon im voraus den Film. Und man könnte sagen, den Film als Sprachfilm und auch als Stummfilm. Und im Stummfilm gibt es ja Zwischentitel.

Die Inserts spielen genau die Rolle des Erzählers [...]. Es kann sein, um zu zeigen, daß Kleist den Film vorweggenommen hat; sowohl den Tonfilm, als auch den Stummfilm. (p.119)

According to Rohmer his intention was to preserve what he identifies as the objectivity of Kleist's writing – a critical distance which has sometimes led commentators to detect a prototype of Brechtian estrangement in Kleist's prose style. It is perhaps worth noting in passing that amongst Brecht's many film plans is a brief, very brief, sketch for an adaptation of *Die Marquise von O...:*

Die Marquise von O...

Weiß nicht wer sie geschwängert hat. Der Bursche des Offiziers stellt sich als Vater vor. (Brecht, 1969, p.654)

In general, however, Rohmer translates this distance or objectivity not into linguistic equivalents but rather visual ones, with the help of renowned cameraman Nestor Almendros, who shot the film as a sequence of what one critic has termed ' *tableaux* inspired by a study of the paintings of the period' (Borchardt, 1984, p.130). Rohmer himself describes it in the following terms:

Ich möchte gern so filmen, wie Kleist erzählt. Das ist meine Absicht. Aber vielleicht ist das ganz schwierig und ich weiß nicht, ob es mir gelungen ist. Ich möchte die Objektivität von Kleists Stil bewahren. Und man hat gesagt, ich weiß nicht wer, Kleist erzählt wie ein Erzähler, der den Rücken zum Publikum dreht. Deshalb ist die Kamera ziemlich weit von den Schauspielern entfernt. Es gibt keine Nahaufnahme. Die Personen sieht man, wie in den Gemälden der Epoche, nicht von nahem. (1979b, p.118)

Angela Dalle Vacche examines the painterliness of Rohmer's adaptation in her essay 'Painting thoughts, listening to images', in which she analyses in painstaking detail, and with excellent illustrative evidence, the sources for the composition of many of the scenes in the film in paintings of Kleist's age:

Rohmer transcends the opposition of word and image in The Marquise von O... *, [...] the polarities of word and image, literature and painting, undergo a reversal as powerful as the joining of opposites in an oxymoron.* (Vacche, 1993, pp.2–3)

In the light of Rohmer's renowned fondness for the spoken and written word she concludes that this film was blessed by an 'intense compatibility between Kleist's pictorialism and Rohmer's literariness' (p.6). Citing French painters including David, Fragonard and Greuze as possible sources alongside Kersting and Friedrich, Vacche argues that Rohmer – like many of the painters of the late eighteenth and early nineteenth centuries – masks emotional intensity and social tensions with a smooth, neo-classical or studiedly Romantic surface, what she terms 'an obscure feeling of unrest growing underneath the call to public morality'. (p.11)

Vacche concludes that Rohmer's achievement is that rare synthesis of German thought and French vision:

> *Rohmer's images make visible the invisible. In comparison to the rest of her family, the Marquise, who undergoes the most intense degree of stress, speaks very little. But despite her silence, her thoughts are not concealed; she conveys them when we see her holding a paintbrush in mid-air, pacing her room with a small book in her hand, doing a little embroidery, or sitting in her garden in a halo of light. These moments of silent reflection and psychological intimacy are made most eloquent by the absence of music – an art form which, for Rohmer, combines the abstractions of literature and the sensuousness of the visual arts and which he consistently leaves out of his films in order to push to an extreme the dialectic of word and image, to underscore his use of painting as inner speech and of the word as theatrical prop. (p.12)*

8 Rohmer's fidelity

The pitfalls of fidelity have been touced on in Section 3 above. Given the nature of Rohmer's adaptation and his bold assertion that he intended to follow Kleist's text ' *Wort für Wort* ', to film '*wie Kleist erzählt*', it is hardly surprising that the voluminous literature on his *Marquise von O...* should concentrate on the 'discourse of fidelity'. Rohmer's fastidious efforts to be faithful to Kleist have not, however, earned him unqualified praise, as witnessed by the disapproval of Pauline Kael. In *Monthly Film Bulletin* Jonathan Rosenbaum, in what is generally a positive review of the film, challenges the director's ingenuousness in approaching Kleist's *Novelle* as if it were a ready-made screenplay:

Starting from the premise that language is transparent [...] Rohmer is brought quite logically to the operating principle that Kleist's novella is 'adaptable' simply because its basic components are the imaginary constructs perceived through its language (plot, settings, characters, events, themes, etc). (Rosenbaum, 1976, p.253)

However, it becomes clear from Rohmer's meticulous notes on his method that he was alive to the needs and constraints of a cinema audience. These considerations allowed him to justify two not insubstantial changes which appear to run counter to his avowed fidelity:

Es mag befremdlich sein, daß wir uns gegen unsere erklärte Absicht, so nah wie möglich am Text zu bleiben, die Freiheit genommen haben, die Umstände der Vergewaltigung der Heldin zu verändern: Sie wird nicht in Ohnmacht sondern im Schlaf vergewaltigt. In der Tat schien uns eine einfache kinematographische Ellipse nur mit äußerster Behutsamkeit jene drei berühmten Pünktchen belegen zu können, die hier die Erzählung unterbrechen. Im Unterschied zum Leser der Erzählung, dessen Vorstellungskraft wendiger und dessen Denkvermögen abstrakter ist, muß der Filmzuschauer diese leeren Bilder ausstatten, die nicht zu jenen passen, die ihm vorher oder nachher gezeigt werden. Unsere Lösung wird hoffentlich verhindern, daß man sich während des Films Fragen nach dem 'Wie' der Sache stellt, die vom eigentlichen Gegenstand ablenken würden. Und damit diese mehr betrachtet wird – ebenso wie die Freiheit, die Kleist allen psychologischen Interpretationen einräumt, haben wir diese Veränderung am Anfang vorgenommen. Sonst hätte die Gefahr bestanden, daß die Marquise wie eine Verrückte oder eine Heuchlerin erschienen wäre, und ihre Gestalt hätte dadurch an Leidenschaft und Tiefe verloren. Dieser kleine Eingriff macht beides möglich: den außergewöhnlichen Charakter der Geschichte und ihre Glaubwürdigkeit zu wahren. (1979a, p.114)

Second, and perhaps more surprising, is the decision to divide the Count's story of the swan into two parts, placing the conclusion at the end of the film and thereby allowing him to regain his place in her affections through a mixture of poetry and gallantry rather than time, money and expediency as is the case in the text. Rohmer explains this narrative intervention as follows:

> *Dann habe ich die Szene, den Text über den Schwan verschoben.*
> *Und ich meinte, es wäre interessant, am Ende des Films einen sehr*
> *schönen Text von Kleist selbst zu haben. Und die Episode, diese*
> *Erzählung über den Schwan ist etwas sehr Schönes.* (1979b, p.117)

There are, moreover, other not insubstantial changes to Kleist's story. The raw violence of the foiled rape and the passion of the reconciliation between father and daughter are absent from the film, Leopardo is introduced as a suspect in the rape of the Marquise at an early stage and, in the final scene, the Marquise herself also makes an unequivocal gesture of reconciliation prompted by the Count's story-telling. Rohmer has also added a jarring passage of dialogue in which the Marquise protests that whoever may appear on ' *dem gefürchteten Dritten*', it could not possibly be the Count. He, she claims, ' *ist der einzige, den man wirklich nicht verdächtigen kann*. These instances are not cited in order to suggest that Rohmer has not kept to his word, but rather to demonstrate the kind of compromises that even the most ostensibly faithful adaptation can feel obliged to make in transposing a work of prose fiction onto the screen within the framework of a genre such as the historical costume drama.

In her book *Re-viewing Kleist: The discursive construction of authorial subjectivity in West German Kleist films* Mary Rhiel views these compromises more critically. From a feminist position she reads them as part of Rohmer's overall strategy for transforming *Die Marquise von O...* into 'a realist text, complete with a positive heroine' (p.47). Examining Rohmer's view of himself as a 'stand-in' for Kleist (p.26), his inclusion of a narrative frame (pp.28–30), and the various ways in which his modifications create closure where Kleist had opted for openness and ambiguity, she argues that Rohmer's slavish adherence to the text foregrounds Kleist the author as an omnipotent, cohesive presence and thereby undermines the radical modernity of the text, its irony, complexity and antagonisms:

> *Rohmer achieves this by having created a stable positionality from which to address the spectator, a position constructed in and through the authorial figure of Kleist. Formative of this discourse is the notion that the author's consciousness, layed bare in an exact reproduction of the text, will provide the viewer with the opportunity to reflect upon the moral of the story. There is little reflection on the extent to which one can be sure about representing some ultimate truth about the consciousness of the author. In* Die Marquise von O..., *the figure of the author has in fact acted as the narrative glue, a glue which binds the spectator to the image in a way that upholds the fiction of the author-father.* (Rhiel, p.45)

It is compromises and distortions of the kind condemned by Rhiel that Hans Jürgen Syberberg adroitly sidesteps in his adaptation of the same material by presenting the entire text, ' *Wort für Wort*', as a three-and-a-half-hour recitation.

9 Syberberg's *Die Marquise von O...*

Although this is not the place to examine this enigmatic film in detail, it is worth highlighting the general principles underpinning Syberberg's approach to *Die Marquise von O...* for the light they shed both on the problem of fidelity and the notion that ' *man "verfilmt" ja nicht ein Buch, sondern man setzt sich mit einem Buch auseinander*' (Schütte, 1984, p.14).

Syberberg began what developed into an intensive ten-year collaboration with the actress Edith Clever in 1982, when she appeared in his *Parsifal* film. Spurred on by her enthusiasm for Kleist, they proceeded to make the three Kleist adaptations mentioned at the outset: *Penthesilea* (1987), *Die Marquise von O...* (1989), and *Ein Traum was sonst?* (1995). In all of these films Clever is the sole actress, playing all of the roles in an extended monologue performed on a studio stage with minimal props. The resulting films are meditative, measured, and intensely dramatic in both delivery and gesture. All three Kleist monologues began life as stage productions premiered at the Hebbel-Theater in Berlin. In essence these films, shot for financial reasons on video rather than celluloid, are recorded stage performances, documented in a painstakingly Brechtian manner.

This Brechtian documentation of the process of transformation of text onto stage and screen is the key to understanding Syberberg's method in adapting Kleist's *Die Marquise von O...*, which he reads as an authentic record of the lost world in which its author lived. In accordance with the director's speculative interpretation of Kleist's Penthesilea and Marquise as sisters-in-kind – indeed as different aspects of Kleist's own character – he has Clever twice recite the final lines of *Penthesilea* before embarking on her recitation of *Die Marquise von O...* . This estrangement of the *Novelle* is heightened by a sequence of black and white photographs which precede Clever's monologue in the manner of opening credits, and which consists entirely of various photographs of the interior and exterior of the studio in Spandau where the film was shot. These images are accompanied by aircraft noise from the planes approaching nearby Tegel airport, an acoustic reminder of the conditions of production. The same sound subsequently punctuates the rest of the film at irregular intervals. Syberberg restricts these overtly Brechtian effects, which place Clever's recitation of Kleist's text firmly in the here and now, to the opening minutes of the film, returning to them only during the closing credits.

During the first section of Clever's recitation from *Die Marquise von O...* itself – up to and including the rape – Syberberg superimposes onto the image of Clever on stage photographs of open landscapes and, more significantly in the light of the film's political programme, ruined buildings in 1945. During this sequence, which coincides with the chaotic battle scenes in Kleist's text, Syberberg constructs a semi-documentary historical context for the action of Kleist's *Novelle,* polemically locating it against a back-drop of the immediate post-war years by using photographic material in the manner of Brechtian projections. Syberberg's photographs of the site of the once-glorious Schloß Friedersdorf (the castle which Kleist visited shortly before his death) and archive shots of the destruction of Schloß Berlin after 1945 were – according to Syberberg at least – interpreted by German audiences as a political provocation rather than, as the director

46

intended, elegiac fragments of a meditation on the lost world of Prussian aristocracy, the memory of which he sees preserved in Kleist's text:

> *Dem Kleistschen Text haben wir die Bilder von Schloß Friedersdorf im Oderbruch hinzugefügt, dazu die Bilder vom Schloß Berlin, dem Stadtschloß in seinem ruinösen Zustand, wie es bis 1950 vor seiner Sprengung existierte. Es sind die Orte, an denen die Geschichte nun stattfindet. Beide Häuser, geschichtsträchtig, existieren nicht mehr. Sie wurden durch den letzten Krieg beschädigt, durchaus restaurierbar, mehr als vieles, das wieder aufgebaut wurde, aber beide Häuser wurden radikal beseitigt, dem Erdboden gleichgemacht. Auf dem Platz des einen sind heute ein Fußballplatz und neue Siedlerhäuschen der Bodenreform, und auf dem anderen steht der Palast der Republik der DDR.* (Clever and Syberberg, 1989, p.6)

Both buildings, Syberberg argues, were destroyed by the East German authorities for ideological reasons – to eradicate the last traces of Prussian society. It is this argument which lends weight to an interpretation of the Marquise's rape in Syberberg's film as a controversial analogy for the 'rape' of Germany by the Allies in 1945, and by the Red Army in particular. Although Syberberg restricts his photographic interpolations to the opening and closing sequences of the film, Clever continues to recite Kleist's words in front of a huge backcloth depicting rubble and, in the second half of the film, a watercolour of the Friedersdorf estate before its demise, which stands in for the Marquise's country retreat.

Syberberg's *Marquise von O...* and in particular the book he compiled to accompany it, which contains texts by members of the von der Marwitz family that owned Schloß Friedersdorf, are both intended to preserve and celebrate the memory of the lost 'golden age' of Prussia, the loss of which Syberberg has repeatedly mourned since   *Nacht* (1985), his first monologue film with Clever. To accompany his own essay in the book to the film he quotes Fontane's well-known remark that ' *Wer den Adel abschaffen wollte, schaffte den letzten Rest von Poesie aus der Welt*', and celebrates the Prussian virtues of ' *Ehre*' and '*Pflicht*' (Clever and Syberberg, 1989, pp.10–11).

The castle, as a metaphor rather than a specific building, is the central utopian image in the film. In his accompanying texts Syberberg variously describes the castle as ' *das Urbild des Traums von Labyrinth und Märchen, der menschlichen Kultur*' (p.45) and as ...

> ... *[eine] Symbiose aus Tieren, Menschen, Pflanzen, Erde, Wald, Seen und Himmel, eines ländlichen Staatsorganismus, einer übersichtlichen Gemeinschaft, ehrendes und dienendes Modell im Kleinen, einer utopischen Weltrealisation vor dem technischen Massenzeitalter und seiner materialistisch bestimmten Selbstverwirklichung, die örtlich und zeitlich ins Planetarische flieht.* (p.69)

For Syberberg's utopian community, art was the indispensable, sanctifying crown of life, and it is this function with which Syberberg attempts to reinvest it in his film. His *Marquise von O...* is thus, like Rohmer's before it, an examination of the society which produced the `btext. However, whilst Rohmer's aim is to examine psychological patterns and social rituals, Syberberg appropriates Kleist's text for overtly political ends. His film is a lament, an elegy for a lost world:

> *Die Vertiefung in Kleist als Beispiel und Maßstab vieler Irrtümer auf dem gegenwärtigen Theater und Anlaß für neue Überlegungen, sowie jener, daß jedem Volk seine besondere Rolle unter den anderen zugemessen ist und was diese wohl sei und wie man damit umgeht. Damit war die sich immer erneuernErkenntnis einer Ästhetik aus der Logik der Kunst nötig. [...] Dieses Kleist-Erlebnis führte schon wie der* Parsifal *weit weg von den musealen Interpretationszwängen des Protests gegen die weggeschmuggelten Urheber zu den Quellen selbst und ließ deutlich meßbar erkennen, woher wir kommen und wie weit entfernt von unserem Selbst wir waren.* (Syberberg, 1992, n.p.)

10 'An affinity for Kleist'

The text from which the preceding remarks of Syberberg are taken is entitled *'Ein autobiographischer Rückblick*. Paradoxically it is the very subjectivity of Rohmer's and Syberberg's readings which emerges most conspicuously from their ostensibly faithful, at times even slavish adherence to the letter of *Die Marquise von O...* . This comes as no surprise given Kleist's status as a 'culture hero' for the New German Cinema (Elsaesser, p.89). Helma-Sanders Brahms, herself director of two Kleist films, summed up the appeal of both the writer and his works as follows:

> *Ever since school I have felt an affinity for Kleist. He is so contradictory, awkward and extreme; qualities which somehow for me represent Germany. What fascinates me about Kleist is the huge gap between the demands he makes on himself and others, and the reality of his life.* (Elsaesser, p.88)

'Contradictory, awkward and extreme' are epithets that could be applied to Syberberg and Rohmer. The explicit kinship felt in both cases between filmmaker and writer goes some way to explaining their humility in the face of the text, a submissiveness which seems to run counter to their outspokenly independent voices. However, this sense of affinity with an outspoken radical also provides them with a vindication of the intractable subjectivity of their readings of one and the same text.

Rohmer claims that his aim was to use *Die Marquise...* as a shooting script with detailed stage directions. The result is a meticulous costume drama which aspires in the main to probe the text in its historical context. Syberberg, on the other hand, makes no attempt to find visual equivalents for the written word, choosing instead to have the entire text recited as a monologue, a document of a reading of the text in the present, rather than a historical drama. Both directors also claim to be exploring the enigma of Kleist the man and artist. Despite the obvious differences in their approaches to the text it is thus clear that it is not only Edith Clever that the two films have in common. Both directors demonstrate through their *Marquise* films that they are enthusiastic advocates of the capacity of *Literaturverfilmung* to reanimate canonical texts in order that they speak directly to a contemporary audience without losing sight of their status as literary and historical documents.

Bibliography

Borchardt E, 'Eric Rohmer's *Marquise von O...* and the theory of the German Novella' in: *Literature/Film Quarterly,* vol. 12, no. 2, pp.129–130 (1984)

Brauerhoch A, 'Der Autorenfilm: Emanzipatorisches Konzept oder autoritäres Modell' in: Hoffmar, Hilmar, Schobert W, (eds), *Abschied von Gestern: Bundesdeutscher Film der Sechziger und Siebziger Jahre.* (Frankfurt am Main, Deutsches Filmmuseum, pp.154–165, 1991)

Brecht B, 'Pläne für Filme' in: *Werkausgabe, Supplementarband: Texte für Filme II: Exposés, Szenarien,* ed. by Gersch W and Hecht W (Frankfurt am Main, Suhrkamp, pp.653–657, 1969)

Clever E and Syberberg H J, *Die Marquise von O... (... vom Süden nach dem Norden verlegt)* (Berlin, Frankfurt, Hebbel-Theater, Schauspiel Frankfurt, 1989)

Elsaesser T, *The New German Cinema: A history* (Houndmills, London, BFI Macmillan, 1989)

Gerlach J, 'Rohmer, Kleist, and The Marquise of O... .' in: *Literature/Film Quarterly,* vol. 8, no. 2, pp.84–91 (1980)

Gow G, 'Die Marquise von O...' in: *Films and Filming,* vol. 23, no. 3, pp.33–34 (1976)

Kleist H, von *Sämtliche Erzählungen* (Stuttgart, Reclam, 1984)

Kluge A, *Bestandsaufnahme: Utopie Film* (Frankfurt am Main, Zweitausendeins, 1983)

Milne T, 'Die Marquise von O...' in: *Sight and Sound,* vol. 46, no. 1, pp.54–55 (1976/77)

Michener C, 'New York Film Festival Preview: Charles Michener on *The Marquise von O...*' in: *Film Comment,* vol. 12, no. 5, p.36 (1976)

Orr C, 'The discourse on adaptation' in: *Wide Angle*, 2, pp.72–6 (1984)

Rentschler E, (ed) *German film and literature: Adaptations and transformations* (New York & London, Methuen, 1986)

Richter H, *Filmgegner von heute – Filmfreunde von morgen* (Frankfurt am Main, Fischer, 1981)

Rohmer E, 'Anmerkungen zur Inszenierung' in: Heinrich von Kleist, *Die Marquise von O...: Mit Materialien und Bildern aus dem Film von Eric Rohmer* (Frankfurt am Main, Insel, pp.111–114, 1979a)

————. 'Interview mit Eric Rohmer' in: Heinrich von Kleist, *Die Marquise von O...: Mit Materialien und Bildern aus dem Film von Eric Rohmer,* (Frankfurt am Main, Insel, pp.115–124, 1979b)

Rosenbaum J, 'Die Marquise von O...' *Monthly Film Bulletin* vol. 43, no. 515, pp.253 (1976)

Rhiel M, *Re-viewing Kleist: The discursive construction of authorial subjectivity in West German Kleist films* (New York etc, Peter Lang, 1991)

Ruttmann W, 'Kunst und Kino' in: Georgen J, *Walter Ruttmann: Eine Dokumentation* (Berlin, Freunde der deutschen Kinemathek, n.d.)

Sandford J, *The New German Cinema* (London, Eyre Methuen, 1981)

Schütte W, 'Gespräch mit Danièle Huillet und Jean-Marie Straub' in: *Klassenverhältnisse: Von Danièle Huillet und Jean-Marie Straub nach dem Amerika-Roman 'Der Verschollene' von Franz Kafka* (Frankfurt am Main, Fischer, pp.37–58, 1984)

Syberberg H J, *Ein autobiographischer Rückblick durch Stationen der deutschen Filmgeschichte nach dem letzten Kriege,* unpublished essay (1992)

Vacche A D, 'Painting thoughts, listening to images: Eric Rohmer's The Marquise of O... .' in: *Film Quarterly,* vol. 46, no. 4, pp.2–15 (1993)

4 | Selbst- und Fremdbetrachtungen bei Fassbinder. Eine exemplarische Analyse von *Angst essen Seele auf*

Guido Rings
Anglia Polytechnic University

1 Fassbinder und der Neue Deutsche Film

Es ist mehr als Respekt gegenüber einem professionellen Filmemacher, wenn der Drehbuchautor, Regisseur, Schauspieler und Produzent Rainer Werner Fassbinder im Todesjahr 1982 von der internationalen Presse als Modellfigur des Neuen Deutschen Kinos hervorgehoben wird. Schütte (1982, S.10) resümiert die Kritik exemplarisch: „Wenn man sich den Neuen Deutschen Film allegorisch als Mensch imaginierte, so wäre Kluge sein Kopf, Herzog sein Wille, Wenders sein Auge, Schlöndorff seine Hände und Füße [...], aber Fassbinder wäre sein Herz gewesen, die lebendige Mitte."[15] Die Allegorie vom „Herz des Neuen Deutschen Films" hält sich auch über den von der Presse gefeierten zehnjährigen Todestag Fassbinders hinaus. [16]

Ein Grund für diese Hochschätzung als „Motor des deutschen Films" (Feldmann, 1982, S.14) ist zunächst die außerordentliche Quantität der Produktionen. Mit umgerechnet 50 Filmen für Kino und Fernsehen in gerade einmal 13 Jahren überragt er nicht nur jeden anderen Regisseur des Neuen Deutschen Kinos, er stellt auch einen internationalen Rekord auf, der schon des häufigeren zur Reflektion über die Grenzen des Möglichen Anlaß gegeben hat. Trotz des hohen Produktionsdruckes

---

15 Vgl. auch Schütte (1983, S.14).
16 Vgl. die WZ vom 30.5.1992 (S. 5) und die *Frankfurter Rundschau* vom 10.6.1992 (S.8).

gehören zahlreiche Fassbinderfilme zu den besten Arbeiten des Neuen Deutschen Films. Die ab 1970 gesammelte Menge an Filmpreisen führt hierfür wohl den besten Beleg: Bereits die zweite Spielfilmproduktion, *Katzelmacher,* in der erstmals ein Gastarbeiter im Mittelpunkt steht, erhält für Drehbuch, Kameraführung und darstellerische Leistung den Deutschen Filmpreis in Gold. In den folgenden Jahren werden zahlreiche weitere Filme preisgekrönt, der internationale Durchbruch gelingt Fassbinder jedoch mit *Angst essen Seele auf,* der 1974 auf dem Festival in Cannes mit dem Preis der Internationalen Filmkritik und dem Preis der christlichen Jury ausgezeichnet wird. Es folgen weitere nationale und internationale Auszeichnungen.

Neben Quantität und Qualität ist die Vielfältigkeit von Fassbinders Produktionen unbestreitbar: die Bandbreite reicht von Kurzfilmen und Theaterinszenierungen in München, Berlin, Bremen, Nürnberg und Frankfurt über zahlreiche Fernseharbeiten bis zu der dominanten Spielfilmproduktion, deren Gestaltung auch innerhalb kürzester Zeiträume außerordentlich variiert, *„from the extreme stylisation of* Die bitteren Tränen der Petra von Kant (1972) *to the austerely elegant black and white photography of* Effi Briest (1974) [...] *and the bold colour expressionism of* Martha (1973)" (Roud, 1980, S.338). Fassbinder beweist sein Talent in Filmen wie *Angst essen Seele auf* als Regisseur, Drehbuchautor, Darsteller und Produzent, wird darüber hinaus aber oft auch als Komponist, Ausstatter und Cutter tätig. Zudem kann er auf Multitalente in der teilweise mit ihm zusammenlebenden und über Jahre hinaus weitgehend konsistenten „antitheater"-Gruppe zurückgreifen, wobei insbesondere auf Darsteller wie Hanna Schygulla, [17] Irm Hermann, Ingrid Caven, Wolfgang Schenk und Ulli Lommel zu verweisen ist. Bei den Dreharbeiten zu *Angst essen Seele auf* erlebt Brigitte Mira (Lorenz, 1995, S.334) das „antitheater" als „feste Crew", die sich ihr gegenüber aber schnell öffnet.

Im Mittelpunkt der negativen Kritik an Fassbinders Werk stehen nicht selten die Auswirkungen des extremen Produktionsdrucks auf das „antitheater." Fassbinders „Arbeitswut" und „Produktionsfanatismus", die dauerhaft zu wenig Schlaf und hohem Drogenkonsum führten, werden

---

[17]   Schygulla erhält für ihre Rolle in *Lili Marleen* 1981 den Bambi.

als Gründe für den frühen Tod des Filmemachers und auch für die zahlreichen Krisen in der Gruppe angeführt. Henrichs (1973, S.15) zitiert exemplarisch die Vorwürfe der in Fassbinders Monumentalwerk führenden Schauspielerinnen an der stereotypen Gestaltung zentraler femininer Filmrollen: „Ich mußte immer zickig sein (Irm Hermann)", „Ich spielte immer die gleiche Rolle – die verlorene Unschuld (Hanna Schygulla)". Und Ingrid Caven, zeitweilig Fassbinders Ehefrau, resümiert: „Ob es nun *Wildwechsel* ist, *Liliom* oder *Der Händler der vier Jahreszeiten* – es ist immer die gleiche widerliche Geschichte von dem bemitleidenswerten Märtyrer-Mann und dem bösen Weib." Henrichs nimmt solche, im Kontext des ersten hohen Produktionsdrucks der frühen 70er Jahre getätigten Aussagen als Grundlage für seine These von einer „Versteinerung des ‚antitheaters'" mit einer stereotypen „Inszenierung wie am Fließband (1973, S.10)". Eine solche These ist freilich weder vor dem Hintergrund der 70er Jahre noch rückblickend auf das Gesamtwerk Fassbinders haltbar. Die Rollenetikettierung Cavens paßt in einer solch simplifizierenden Form weder auf die Mehrheit der nicht genannten frühen Produktionen – *Angst essen Seele auf* ist ein gutes Gegenbeispiel – noch auf die folgenden Werke. Die Wiederverwendung gleicher Schauspieler in bewährten Rollen ist keineswegs eine Fassbinderinvention, und die geringe Bereitschaft zur Reflektion von Rollen kann auch als Stärke Fassbinders gewertet werden. Die innerhalb eines gewissen Rahmens weitgehend den Darstellern überlassene Interpretation der Rollen trägt zu einer natürlichen Spontaneität oder Authentizität der Filmcharaktere bei und spart zudem Zeit bei den Dreharbeiten.

Dies leitet über zur Frage nach dem thematischen Schwerpunkt des Gesamtwerkes, die innerhalb der Diskussion um Fassbinders politische Ausrichtung und der Vielfalt der Produktionen nicht einfach zu beantworten ist. Wie viele bekannte Filmemacher des Neuen Deutschen Kinos ist er ein äußerst scharfer Sozialkritiker, angelehnt an die Kritik der 68er Generation gegenüber Establishment und bürgerlichen Mentalitäten. Er thematisiert Identitätsprobleme des modernen Menschen in einer nach kapitalorientierten sozialen Normen strukturierten Gesellschaft, die sich in seinen Filmen überwiegend im Nachkriegsdeutschland des 20ten Jahrhunderts manifestiert. Wie in zahlreichen Neuen Deutschen Filmen sind auch seine Protagonisten Außenseiter, die oft mehr unbewußt als bewußt die geltenden Normen verletzen und so mit der Umgebung in Konflikt geraten. Thematisiert werden die Normzwänge und – untrennbar hiermit verbunden – die Angst der Außenseiterprotagonisten vor den zahlreichen Formen der Sanktionierung von Normverletzungen, bzw. letztendlich vor der dem vorgegebenen Normenschema nicht entsprechenden eigenen Identität, die eine latente Hauptquelle für die Normkonflikte ist. Fassbinders „radikal naive, fast biblisch vereinfachte" Utopie einer künftigen Gesellschaft resümiert Märthesheimer (1982, S.15) denn auch wie folgt: Hier „würden die Menschen frei miteinander umgehen können, frei von Armut und Not, frei von Unterdrückung und Bevormundung, frei vor allem von jeder Art von Angst. Die Angst eines jeden vor jedem [...] und insbesondere die Angst eines jeden vor sich selbst. [...] Die angstfreie Gesellschaft der Zukunft würde nur noch Freie kennen." Bei dem hier zu besprechenden Film, *Angst essen Seele auf,* erscheint das Hauptthema wie bei einigen anderen Produktionen des Neuen Deutschen Kinos bereits im Titel.[18] Aber auch wenn die Angst nicht explizit im Filmtitel geführt wird, ist sie in den meisten Fassbinderfilmen allgegenwärtig als „Angst vor Liebesverlust, Angst auch vor Liebe, Angst vor den nur oberflächlich unterdrückten, übermächtigen Gewaltimpulsen in der eigenen Seele, Angst vor einem Versiegen der künstlerischen Produktivität, Angst vor Anpassung, vor Identitätsverlust, vor Verbeugung und Verkrümmung und Verkrüppelung angesichts der bestehenden Machtverhältnisse, Angst vor der eigenen Angst (Märthesheimer, 1982, S.15)". Nicht zufällig sind die von einer oder mehreren der genannten Angstformen geplagten Außenseiter-protagonisten in zwei der frühen Spielfilmproduktionen Gastarbeiter, wobei Fassbinder selber den Griechen Jorgos in *Katzelmacher* und sein langjähriger Freund El Hedi Ben Salem den Marokkaner Ali in *Angst essen Seele auf* spielt. Berlinger (1992, S.19) verweist auf den Umstand, daß der erste Freund des homosexuellen Rainer Fassbinder ein griechischer Gastarbeiter ist, der von Fassbinders Mutter abgelehnt wird, weil er „kein der deutschen Sprache mächtiger Mann und vor allem kein Akademiker ist". Der spätere Regisseur kennt die Lebenssituation von

---

18   Vgl. Wenders *Die Angst des Tormanns beim Elfmeter* (1972), Kückelmanns *Die Angst ist ein zweiter Schatten* und Kratischs *Henry Angst* (1980).

Gastarbeitern aber auch aus seiner Tätigkeit als Eintreiber von Außenständen im Dienst seines Immobilien vermietenden Vaters. In Köln lernt er die beengten Wohnverhältnisse von Gastarbeitern, deren finanzielle Probleme und vor allem die Diskriminierung durch die deutsche Umgebung kennen (Berlinger, 1992, S.20) – Aspekte des „Gastarbeiterproblems" also, die in der zeitgenössischen bundesdeutschen Presse keine, oder allenfalls eine marginale Rolle spielen. Es ist vielmehr als Gegenreaktion auf die offizielle Darstellung des „Gastarbeiterproblems" zu werten, wenn die Außenseiterprotagonisten des Neuen Deutschen Films mitunter Gastarbeiter sind. [19] Der Aufgriff dieses Themas in *Katzelmacher* und *Angst essen Seele auf* ist entgegen einer These Henrichs (1973, S.15) weit mehr als eine „höchst private Auseinandersetzung Fassbinders mit seinen eigenen Problemen". Der Erfolg der Filme ist vielmehr darauf zurückzuführen, daß Fassbinder eine Abstraktion seiner persönlichen und der in der „antitheater"-Gruppe erfahrenen Probleme auf universalmenschliche Konfliktpotentiale gelungen ist. Darüber hinaus bleibt *Angst essen Seele auf* ein zentraler Beitrag eines international renommierten Filmemachers, der das Deutschlandbild – und hier insbesondere die Zugänge zur Ausländerfeindlichkeit in Deutschland – entscheidend mitgeprägt haben dürfte. Nicht zufällig bewertet die Kommission des „film dienstes" (1974, S.11) *Angst essen Seele auf* als „sehenswerten Film gegen Mißachtung von Rassen, Alter und Außenseiterschicksale".

2 Gastarbeiterzustrom und Fremdenfeindlichkeit

Die realhistorische Folie von *Angst essen Seele auf* ist eine im Kontext des sogenannten Wirtschaftswunders zunächst staatlich sehr geförderte, mit Blick auf die Rezession der Jahre 1966/67 und am Vorabend der Rezession von 1973 aber mit zunehmender Skepsis bis hin zu Fremdenfeindlichkeit betrachtete Masseneinwanderung von „Gastarbeitern". „Gastarbeiter" ist eine nicht-amtliche im öffentlichen Sprachgebrauch der sechziger und siebziger Jahre aber sehr verbreitete Bezeichnung für Ausländer, die zu temporärer Arbeit in Deutschland von staatlichen Behörden angeworben wurden. Der Terminus betont

---

19 Sanders (1985, S.136) verweist exemplarisch auf die genannten Fassbinderfilme, auf Sohrab Shahid Saless *In der Fremde* (1975) und auf Helma Sanders *Shirins Hochzeit* (1975).

die zeitliche Begrenzung des Aufenthaltes, denn „Gast ist nur wer nicht auf Dauer bleibt" (Bade, 1993, S.394).

Der Mitte der fünfziger Jahre einsetzende erhebliche ökonomische Aufschwung mit Anstiegen im Bruttosozialprodukt von zeitweilig 9,5% im Jahresdurchschnitt, hohen Exportüberschüssen der deutschen Industrie und konstanter Erweiterung der Produktion führt zunächst zu einem hohen Arbeitskräftebedarf. Dieser Bedarf vergrößert sich noch durch die Verlängerung der Ausbildungsdauer, die Verkürzung der Arbeitszeit und den Eintritt der geburtenschwachen Jahrgänge ins Erwerbsleben. Zudem entzieht der Aufbau der Bundeswehr dem Arbeitsprozeß ab 1955 fast eine halbe Million Wehrpflichtige und Zivilbedienstete. (Vgl. hierzu Herrmann, 1992, S.4.) Die Regierung Adenauer entschließt sich in dieser Situation zur Anwerbung ausländischer Arbeitnehmer. Rechtliche Grundlage werden das deutsch-italienische Abkommen zur Anwerbung und Vermittlung italienischer Arbeitskräfte für die deutsche Wirtschaft (1955), sowie ähnliche bilaterale Vereinbarungen mit Spanien und Griechenland (1960), mit der Türkei (1961), Marokko (1963), Portugal (1964), Tunesien (1965) und Jugoslawien (1968). Durch den Bau der Berliner Mauer versiegt ab 1961 der Flüchtlingsstrom aus der DDR und den deutschen Ostgebieten, aus denen seit Kriegsende rund 14 Millionen Menschen eingewandert sind. Die Notwendigkeit der Anwerbepolitik scheint so bestätigt, und in der Tat haben die deutschen Unternehmer Anfang der 60er Jahre einen sehr hohen Arbeitskräftebedarf, der ohne Immigranten nicht mehr zu decken ist. Im Jahr 1960 übersteigt die Zahl der offenen Stellen erstmalig die der Arbeitslosen, und auch in den Folgejahren kommt es trotz steigender Immigrantenzahlen zu keinem nennenswerten Arbeitskräfteüberschuß.

Dies ändert sich grundlegend mit der Rezession von 1966/67, auf deren Höhepunkt – im Jahr 1967 – über 600.000 Arbeitslose in der offiziellen Statistik geführt werden. Nach nahezu Vollbeschäftigung in den Jahren 1960–62 wirkt dieser Einbruch im Kontext einer neuen Welle des Rechtsradikalismus und den daraus resultierenden Diskussionen um die Einführung von Notstandsgesetzen wie ein Schock, der den in der Nachkriegsgeneration verbreiteten „Glauben an einen unbegrenzten ökonomischen Fortschritt" (Kistler, 1983, S.248) destabilisiert. Die

Reaktion hierauf ist freilich sehr unterschiedlich. Für einen Teil der jüngeren, sogenannten 68er Generation sind die sozioökonomischen Probleme in der Zeit eines sich verschärfenden Kalten Krieges Anlaß, an der materialistischen Verhaltensdisposition ihrer Eltern und dem hierauf basierenden Gesellschaftssystem zu zweifeln. In der Nachkriegsgeneration selber dominiert hingegen eine Tendenz, die Krise auf einige wenige politische Fehlentscheidungen zurückzuführen. Die Anwerbung von Gastarbeitern, die in den siebziger Jahren weitgehend konstant drei Viertel der ausländischen Arbeitnehmer stellen (Bade, 1993, S.395), wird zunehmend als eine solche Fehlentscheidung empfunden, zumal die Immigrantenzahlen nach dem Einbruch von 1967 auf hohem Niveau wieder ansteigen. Im Entstehungsjahr von *Angst essen Seele auf* (1973) erreicht die Zahl ausländischer Arbeitnehmer mit 2.595.000 ihren absoluten Höhepunkt in der Geschichte der alten Bundesrepublik Deutschland (Herrmann, 1992, S.5) – bei einer Gesamtzahl von 3.966.200 (Bundesminister des Innern, 1983, S.7). Außerdem zeichnet sich in der zweiten Hälfte des Jahres 1973 bereits eine neue Rezession ab (Bundesminister des Innern, 1983, S.7). Von 1969 bis 1973 steht ein kontinuierlicher Anstieg der Lebenshaltungskosten (1969: +2,8%; 1970: +3,7%; 1971: +5,4%; 1973: +7%) einer weitgehenden konjunkturellen Stagnation gegenüber (Kistler, 1983, S.310 ff). Ihre Verschärfung durch die Ölpreiskrise und die damit verbundene Gefahr hoher Arbeitslosigkeit veranlassen die Bundesregierung im November 1973 zur Einstellung aller Anwerbeprogramme. Ein drastisches und vor allem dauerhaftes Sinken der Ausländergesamtanzahl ist damit jedoch nicht verbunden. Vielmehr wird der vorläufige Höhepunkt von 4.089.594 im Jahr 1974 schon fünf Jahre später wieder überschritten, da der Anwerbestopp bei den bereits in Deutschland lebenden Gastarbeitern „die Tendenz zu Daueraufenthalt und Familiennachzug fördert" (Bade, 1993, S.396), und auch die Geburtenzahlen deutlich höher liegen. Die unverändert hohe Gesamtzahl der Ausländer trägt im Kontext von Wirtschaftskrisen und hoher Arbeitslosigkeit keineswegs zum Abbau einer Skepsis an Ausländereinwanderung bei, die bereits zu Beginn der Anwerbung verbreitet ist.

Bereits 1960, als die Zahl der in der Bundesrepublik beschäftigten Ausländer noch unter der 300.000-Grenze liegt, ist nach Katsoulis (1984,

S.112) „das Verhalten der Deutschen zu Ausländern durch die Erinnerung an die Fremdarbeiterpolitik des Hitlerfaschismus belastet". Auch Albaladejo y Fuertes (1987, S.78) resümiert, daß „die ausländischen Arbeiter von der deutschen Bevölkerung zunächst als ein ‚notwendiges Übel' angesehen wurden". Solche Ergebnisse stehen in direkter Opposition zu dem von Regierungs- und Unternehmerseite propagierten Bild einer allgemeinen freundlichen Akzeptanz der ersten Gastarbeitergeneration. Als Beleg der offiziellen Geschichtsversion wird bis heute ein Bild verbreitet, in dem der einmillionste Gastarbeiter, ein Portugiese, 1964 beim Willkommensgruß mit einem Moped beschenkt wurde (Herrmann, 1992, S.4). Vor dem Hintergrund neuerer mentalitätshistorischer Untersuchungen bleibt zu hinterfragen, inwieweit solche Bilder die Verhaltensdisposition einer kollektiven Mehrheit wiedergeben. Von einer verbreiteten „Fremdenfeindlichkeit" ist in den Zeiten des wirtschaftlichen Aufschwungs freilich nicht auszugehen;[20] sie entsteht erst im Kontext einer Verschärfung der Arbeitsmarktlage Ende der sechziger und Anfang der siebziger Jahre und richtet sich dann vornehmlich gegen Türken, deren Masseneinwanderung als besonders fremdartig eingestuft wird. (1971 stellen die Türken mit einer Gesamtzahl von 653.000 erstmals den größten Anteil ausländischer Familien in der Bundesrepublik. Das kollektive Bewußtsein einer besonderen Fremdartigkeit der Türken bestätigen Klöpper (1985, S.13) und Andersen (1986, S.32) mit Blick auf *Spiegel-* und *Capital*-Umfragen.) Klöpper (1985, S.13) verweist auf eine Fülle von Verbalinjurien der frühen siebziger Jahre wie „Kümmeltürke", „Kameltreiber" und „Hammelfresser", Ney (1975, S.158ff.) auf Schüleraufsätze einer achten Hauptschulklasse, in der für Gastarbeiter aus südlichen Anwerbeländern die gesamte Vorurteilspalette von „schmutzig", „frech", „Messerstecher" bis hin zum „Schürzenjäger" wieder aufgegriffen wird. Die gängigen Türkenwitze der Zeit verdichten sich hier bis zu einem Feindbild, das die Frustration und Aggression der Krisenzeiten bedingt ableitet. Andererseits zeigt sich gerade in den Schüleraufsätzen eine über das Verständnis der Elterngeneration hinausgehende Sensibilität für die Situation aus der Perspektive der Gastarbeiter, insbesondere für deren Isolation: „Ich würde keinen

---

20   So Albaladejo y Fuertes (1987, S.78) im Gegensatz zu Klöpper (1985, S.13), der in den 60er Jahren von einer „latenten Fremdenfeindlichkeit" ausgeht, die Anfang der 70er zum Durchbruch kommt.

Gastarbeiter heiraten. Nicht, daß ich gegen die Gastarbeiter etwas hätte. [...] Aber man muß auch an die Kinder denken, die man später bekommt. Es würde niemand mit ihnen spielen, weil die Eltern ihre Kinder gegen sie aufgehetzt haben. Meine beiden Brüder dürfen auch nicht mit Gastarbeiterkindern spielen (Gaby X, in: Ney, 1975, S.160)." In München, dem Handlungsort von *Angst essen Seele auf*, und anderen Ballungszentren wie Berlin und Frankfurt provoziert der verstärkte Türkenzuzug den Umzug Tausender deutscher Familien und hinterläßt ganze „Türkengettos". Vor diesen an Wohnqualität schnell verlierenden „kleinen Harlems" warnen Politiker wie der Münchner Oberbürgermeister Hans Jochen Vogel und insbesondere die Presse. Exemplarisch ist *Der Spiegel* (31, 1973), der im Entstehungszeitraum von Fassbinders Film unter dem plakativen Titel „Die Türken kommen – rette sich, wer kann" Städteverfall, Kriminalität und soziale Verelendung moniert. [21]

Die hier reflektierten Abwehrmechanismen gegenüber den „Fremden" wiederholen sich in Krisenzeiten in ähnlichem Ausmaß – zuletzt im Kontext der Masseneinwanderung von Aussiedlern und Asylanten zu Beginn der neunziger Jahre. Unabhängig von solchen Erscheinungen existiert in der Dauerkrise der modernen Industriegesellschaft im Rahmen zunehmender Migration die im Entstehungszeitraum von Angst essen Seele auf dominante Verhaltensdisposition weiter: „Ausländische Arbeiter werden als Belastung für ‚unsere' Gesellschaft, vor allem aber für die ökonomische Sicherheit empfunden; sie nehmen angeblich Arbeitsplätze weg, überfordern den Sozialversicherungsträger und gefährden somit ‚unseren' Wohlstand. Schreckensmeldungen über die Ausländerflut [...] suggerieren die Gefahr vor Überfremdung und vermitteln den Eindruck, daß die Ausländer in Deutschland nur ihren Profit suchen (Albaladejo y Fuertes, 1987, S.78)".

---

21 *Der Spiegel* vom 30.7.1973 widmet den Türkengettos einen elfseitigen Bericht, der die Verdrängung deutscher Familien und deutscher Kultur fokalisiert. Die Parteinahme des Autors gegen weiteren Türkenzuzug wird über den Sprachstil wirkungsvoll unterstützt. Türken „mehren sich redlich", es gibt „Scharen von Illegalen" und die „Türken-Kolonien" werden jährlich durch „ganze Brigaden verstärkt" (S.24).

3 *Angst essen Seele auf*

3.1 *Zur Gastarbeiterproblematik im Film*

Vor dem Regen flüchtet die etwa sechzigjährige verwitwete Putzfrau Emmi in eine Gastwirtschaft, die hauptsächlich von Gastarbeitern besucht wird. Hier fordert sie der etwa zwanzig Jahre jüngere Marokkaner Ali zum Tanz auf. Beide sind einsam: Ali hat keine Kontakte zur deutschen Umgebung, und die Ausländerkneipe, eine Art Refugium vor alltäglicher Ausbeutung, bietet kaum mehr als geringe oberflächliche Konversation und die Möglichkeit, sexuelle Kontakte zu knüpfen. Die von Ali gesuchte Kommunikation ist hier nicht zu finden. Auch Emmi ist nach dem Tod ihres Mannes alleine; die Kinder leben ihr eigenes Leben, mit den Nachbarinnen bleibt es bei oberflächlicher Unterhaltung, und die Arbeitskolleginnen kennen im wesentlichen zwei Gesprächsthemen: das schlechte Vorbild gesellschaftlicher Außenseiter und ihren Wunsch nach Lohnerhöhung. Die Ähnlichkeit ihrer Situation und die Möglichkeit, beieinander die gesuchte Kommunikation zu finden, entdecken die ungleichen Charaktere spätestens bei einem Glas Cognak in Emmis Wohnung. Aus der flüchtigen Begegnung wird Liebe – eine Liebe, die von der Umwelt nicht verstanden und nicht geduldet wird. Nach der Heirat machen Emmis Kinder ihrer Mutter Vorwürfe wegen der Unmoral, der Lebensmittelhändler weigert sich, Ali zu bedienen, Nachbarn und Arbeitskollegen gehen Emmi aus dem Weg und starten Hetzreden,[22] aber die erste Verhaltensweise ist bei allen und der übrigen Umwelt sehr ähnlich: ein verständnisloses Starren auf das ungleiche Paar. Diese Form distanzierter und verengter Betrachtung steht denn auch im Mittelpunkt des Films. Sie kulminiert in einem Wutausbruch Emmis auf der Terrasse eines Gartenlokals („Warum gafft ihr so? Das ist mein Mann, mein Mann!") und leitet über Emmis Entschluß, erst einmal Urlaub machen zu wollen, den Wendepunkt des Films ein.

---

22 Dies entgegen der Darstellung bei Krusche (1991, S. 44), der bereits vor der Heirat „bittere Vorwürfe" der Kinder festzustellen glaubt. Die Heirat ist keine Trotzreaktion gegenüber sozialen Sanktionierungsmaßnahmen, sondern Ausdruck von Normengehorsam. Die Idee der Legalisierung ihrer Beziehung kommt Emmi spontan bei der Klage des Vermieters über Alis unrechtmäßigen Aufenthalt in ihrer Wohnung. Dabei übersieht sie, daß die „Institutionalisierung in Form einer bürgerlichen Ehe" die spießbürgerliche Umgebung auf das schärfste zu provozieren vermag (vgl. KIM (1987, S.149) und (1994, S.28)).

Nach dem Urlaub ist die Umgebung wie gewandelt: Emmis Kinder, der Kaufmann, die Nachbarn und selbst die Arbeitskollegen sind wieder freundlich. Doch dies ist nicht auf einen Anflug von Humanität, sondern auf die Einsicht entgangenen Eigennutzes zurückzuführen. Emmis Sohn braucht die Mutter als Babysitter, der Kaufmann möchte sie als Kundin zurückgewinnen, die Nachbarin benötigt Ali für ihren Möbeltransport, und die Arbeitskolleginnen wollen Solidarität, um Lohnforderungen durchzusetzen, zumal mittlerweile ein anderer Außenseiter gefunden worden ist. Emmi läßt sich und Ali bereitwillig ausbeuten, um wieder eine gewisse soziale Akzeptanz zu erhalten. Als sie jedoch der Perspektive ihrer deutschen Umgebung allzu deutlich folgt, die Ali günstigstenfalls als muskelstrotzenden Exoten akzeptiert und für Kuskus als Mittagessen keinerlei Verständnis hat, zieht Ali sich zu der jungen und attraktiven Besitzerin der Ausländerkneipe zurück. [23] Noch einmal kann der Rezipient auf ein Happy End hoffen, als es Emmi gelingt, ihren Mann in der Ausländerkneipe zum Tanz zu bewegen. Aber das Glück ist nur von kurzer Dauer: Ali bricht an einem Magengeschwür zusammen, das nach Auskunft des Arztes bei Gastarbeitern wegen deren Streßsituation häufig entsteht und immer wieder ausbricht. Mit Emmis Entscheidung, in dieser Auswegslosigkeit bei ihrem Mann bleiben zu wollen, endet der Film in einer für Fassbinder charakteristischen Weise. Freybourg formuliert (1993, S.84): „Das Leitmotto, daß es ‚kein richtiges Leben im falschen‘ gibt, läßt [...] die Lebensläufe zusammenbrechen, läßt sie enden in schleichenden, dann plötzlich implodierenden Katastrophen.“

Die Liebe zwischen einer älteren Putzfrau und einem sehr viel jüngeren Gastarbeiter wird bereits in Fassbinders *Der amerikanische Soldat* (1970) thematisiert. Allerdings erscheint das Thema dort nur über die kurze Erzählung eines Zimmermädchens, der Gastarbeiter Ali ist – wie die Mehrheit der in Deutschland beschäftigten Ausländer – ein Türke, und die Geschichte endet zweifelsfrei tragisch: Die Frau wird ermordet, der Täter jedoch nie gefaßt, denn der die Polizei zu Ali führende Siegelring mit dem eingravierten „A“ reicht als Beweisgrundlage nicht

---

23 Töteberg (1995, S. 30) formuliert, daß „jeder in seinen Kreis aufgenommen wird und dabei immer auch den anderen verrät“. Der Fokus des Films liegt jedoch auf der Integration Alis, deren Forcierung durch Emmi nicht als „Verrat“ betrachtet werden kann, schließlich geht es beiden bei ihrer Beziehung primär um die Überwindung von Einsamkeit, nicht um die kulturelle Identität des anderen.

aus. Alis Gegenargument, „Alle Türken heißen Ali", ist denn auch der Arbeitstitel des hier zu besprechenden Films, dessen Drehbuch Fassbinder im Sommer 1973 fertigstellt und der im September 1973 unter seiner Regie in wenig mehr als vierzehn Tagen in München gedreht wird (Pflaum, 1992, S.34; vgl. auch Töteberg, 1995, S.30, und Krusche, 1991, S.210). Auch an der Produktion ist Fassbinder durch seine eigene Firma Tango-Film beteiligt. Die Hauptrollen besetzen sein damaliger Lebensgefährte, El Hedi Ben Salem, und der über diesen Film wieder an Popularität gewinnende Altstar des Theaters, Brigitte Mira. Mit Rücksicht auf El Hedi Ben Salems marokkanische Abstammung und auf die Umgestaltung des Geschichtsendes frei nach dem Sirkschen Melodrama *All that heaven allows,* vor allem aber mit Blick für das eigentliche Thema des Films fällt die Entscheidung für den endgültigen Titel auf *Angst essen Seele auf.* Dieses mit Bezug auf eine angebliche sprachliche Hilflosigkeit von Immigranten bewußt im Infinitivstil formulierte Motiv umreißt das Thema ungleich prägnanter: Hinter der Liebe der beiden ungleichen Protagonisten steckt eine existenzielle Angst vor den Konsequenzen, die ein mehrfacher Bruch der sozialen Norm mit sich bringen kann. Es handelt sich um die Angst des Außenseiters vor vollständiger Marginalisierung und Einsamkeit. Aber auch die Alternative eines Rückzugs aus der Beziehung ist von Angst besetzt, schließlich führt er doch nur in die Einsamkeit des täglichen Lebens zurück. Der Gastarbeiter Ali und die verwitwete Putzfrau Emmi sind in diesem Sinne Beispiele für eine zutiefst menschliche Angst vor der Einsamkeit, die auf die Situation einer großen Mehrheit der deutschen Bevölkerung, bzw. der Bevölkerung von Industrieländern, und dies nicht nur der siebziger Jahre, übertragen werden kann.

Fassbinders Auswahl des zentralen Außenseiterprotagonisten fällt 1973 nicht zufällig auf einen Gastarbeiter, schließlich sind die Menschen dieser Gruppe Anfang der siebziger Jahre in Deutschland in besonderem Maße isoliert. Im Kontext wachsender Fremdenfeindlichkeit provoziert ihre bloße Anwesenheit vielerorts abfällige Bemerkungen, Ausländerwitze, teilweise Wandschmierereien mit dem Slogan „Ausländer raus!" Vorurteile werden ausgetauscht, intensiviert und sehr oft auch auf Deutsche übertragen, wenn diese sich mit Ausländern einlassen. Nicht zufällig wird *Angst essen Seele auf* ein enger Realitätsbezug bescheinigt: Feldmann (1982, S.14) betrachtet die in

Katzelmacher und *Angst essen Seele auf* thematisierten Probleme als „realistische Sujets", Krusche (1991, S.45) erkennt in letzterem Film eine „genaue Beobachtung alltäglicher Details", Fassbinder (Kim, 1974, S.12) betont den Realismus der einzelnen „Filmpartikel" (der Realitätsbezug der „Geschichte als Ganzes" ist seiner Meinung nach der Textbildung im Kopf des Rezipienten überlassen), und die Kommission des „filmdienstes" (Kim, 1974, S.11) beurteilt ihn als Lehrfilm „gegen Mißachtung von Rassen, Alter und Außenseiterschicksale". Realitätsnähe, publikumswirksame Klarheit und künstlerischer Anspruch sind denn auch die Charakteristiken, die dem Film bei seiner Uraufführung in Frankfurt am 5.3.1974 eine sehr gute Kritik einbringen und noch im selben Jahr bei der Präsentation in Cannes zum internationalen Durchbruch verhelfen. Fassbinder erhält den Fipresci-Preis (internationale Filmkritik) und den der OCIC (Internationales Katholisches Filmbüro) mit der Begründung: „In einem ebenso neuartigen wie wirksamen Filmstil wird exemplarisch ein Fall [...] dargestellt, der die schwierige Lage der Minderheiten und Außenseiter in unserer Zeit deutlich macht und dadurch eine Botschaft der Liebe, des Verstehens und der gegenseitigen Annäherung vermittelt" (Berling, 1992, S.241–2.). Freilich darf Realitätsnähe hier nicht in aristotelischem Sinne als Mimesis realhistorischer Erscheinungen mißverstanden werden.

Fassbinder präsentiert die Gastarbeiterproblematik 1969 in *Katzelmacher* noch mit „Kargheit und lapidarer Wortarmut", in *Angst essen Seele auf* jedoch im „optischen Stil eines hochgestochenen Manierismus" (Feldmann, 1982, S.14). Ein zentraler Grund für den künstlerischen Paradigmawechsel ist seine Überzeugung von der Notwendigkeit einer Produktion publikumswirksamerer Filme nach dem geringen Kassenerfolg von Katzelmacher. Die melodramatische Richtung der neuen Orientierung ist in der intensiven Beschäftigung mit Douglas Sirks Melodramen angelegt. Fassbinder formuliert zu dieser Inspiration: „Nachdem ich zehn Filme gemacht hatte, die sehr persönlich waren, kam der Punkt, wo wir gesagt haben, wir müssen eine Möglichkeit finden, Filme fürs Publikum zu machen – und da kam für mich die Begegnung mit den Filmen und dem Douglas Sirk persönlich. Das war unheimlich wichtig für mich." (Fassbinders Kommentar in der *Süddeutschen Zeitung* vom 8.3.1979). Bereits 1971 formuliert er in seiner Essayistik: „Ich habe sechs Filme von Douglas Sirk gesehen. Es waren die schönsten der Welt dabei" (vgl. Töteberg, 1984, S.24). Im Februar 1971 schließt Fassbinder seinen Essay *Imitation of Life* ab, in dem er sechs Filme von Sirk näher behandelt, darunter *All that heaven allows* (1956). Auch hier wird die soziale Problematik einer Liebe zwischen einer älteren verwitweten Frau und einem sehr viel jüngeren nicht in die Gesellschaft der Frau passenden Mann thematisiert. Fassbinder umreißt die Ausgangssituation in diesem Essay (Töteberg, 1984, S.12) wie folgt: „Jane Wyman ist eine reiche Witwe [Carey Scott], Rock Hudson [Ron Kirby] schneidet ihre Bäume. In Janes Garten blüht ein ‚Liebesbaum', der nur blüht, wo eine Liebe ist, und so wird aus Janes und Rocks zufälligem Zusammentreffen die große Liebe. Rock aber ist fünfzehn Jahre jünger als Jane, und Jane ist total in das gesellschaftliche Leben einer amerikanischen Kleinstadt integriert, Rock ist ein Primitiver, und Jane hat etwas zu verlieren, ihre Freundinnen, das Ansehen, das sie ihrem verstorbenen Mann verdankt, ihre Kinder." Die Grundkonstellation „Sie, er und die Umwelt" (Fassbinder, 1994, S.12), die Klarheit bei der Übereinstimmung von Kameraperspektiven und thematischen Aussagen, vor allem aber die melodramatische Gestaltung des Films überträgt Fassbinder auf *Angst essen Seele auf.*[24] Im Rahmen einer Fokalisierung von Situation und Handlung gehört hierzu die Begrenzung der Figurenanzahl auf kleine überschaubare Gruppen mit leidenden Helden im Mittelpunkt, eine klare Typisierung der Figuren innerhalb des „gut-böse"-Schemas und ein Verzicht auf die Ausführung psychologisch komplexer Eigenschaften zugunsten einer klaren Kontrastierung von Figur und Umwelt. Die grundsätzlich in Exposition, Konfliktentfaltung und -auflösung unterteilbare dramatische Handlung spielt im allgemeinen an wenigen, überschaubaren Orten mit hoch symbolischer Kulisse. Exemplarisch wird der von den Kindern zu Weihnachten geschenkte Fernseher zum Symbol der Inkommunikation Janes, die Musikbox in Alis Kneipe aber zum Symbol von Kommunikation, führt sie Ali und Emmi doch am Anfang und am Ende wieder zusammen (vgl. bereits Mayne, 1977, S.67–8). Auch die Verwendung von Krankheiten als Reflektor menschenfeindlicher

---

24 Dies erlaubt nicht, *Angst essen Seele auf* als „Remake des Sirk-Melodramas" (Limmer, 1981, S.32) zu präsentieren. Limmer übersieht die thematische Nähe zur Erzählung in Fassbinders eigenem Film *Der amerikanische Soldat.* Das Drehbuch zu diesem Film entsteht deutlich vor Fassbinders essayistischer Auseinandersetzung mit Sirk.

sozialer Mißstände ist bei Fassbinder und Sirk sehr ähnlich. Alis Magengeschwür und Careys Kopfschmerzen werden von Ärzten als psychosomatisch diagnostiziert. In ersterem Fall ist der Streß, dem die Gastarbeiter in Deutschland ausgesetzt sind, in letzterem Fall der soziale Druck, den die kleinstädtische Umgebung zwecks Revision des unvernünftigen Liebesverhältnisses auf Carey ausübt, verantwortlich zu machen. *Angst essen Seele auf* endet zudem wie *All that heaven allows* mit der plötzlichen Erkrankung des männlichen Protagonisten, die das soeben wiedergefundene gemeinsame Glück überschattet.

Fassbinder interessiert sich insbesondere für die aus dem Antagonismus von Wunsch und Verbot resultierende emotionale Intensität des Sirkschen Melodramas und dessen Publikumswirksamkeit, die er für die Verbreitung sozialkritischer Inhalte zu nutzen versucht. *All that heaven allows* und andere Filme, aber auch theoretische Schriften hatten angedeutet, daß das Melodrama sich hierzu eignet. So formuliert Elsaesser bereits 1972 (S.14): *„The melodrama [...] seems capable of reproducing more directly than other genres the patterns of domination and exploitation existing in a given society, especially the relation between psychology, morality, and class consciousness, by emphasizing so clearly an emotional dynamic whose social correlative is a network of external forces directed oppressingly inward, and with which the characters themselves unwittingly collide to become their agents."* Nach Roud (1980, S.337) kann ein solchermaßen konstruiertes Melodrama „ *a truer reality than ,realism* " ausdrücken. Das Hollywoodmelodrama der fünfziger Jahre entspricht diesem Verständnis allerdings in den seltensten Fällen, und Fassbinder sieht sich bei *Angst essen Seele auf* genötigt, in einigen signifikanten Punkten von dem Sirkschen Vorbild abzuweichen. Auffällig ist der Verzicht auf ein klares Happy End, mit dem der dramatische Konflikt in den meisten Hollywoodmelodramen, auch in der Mehrheit der Sirkschen Produktionen, aufgelöst wird. Die Charaktere sind in Fassbinders Filmen bei aller Stereotypisierung nicht unveränderlich – im Gegensatz zu der festen Schematisierung von *All that heaven allows* (vgl. Burns, 1995, S.64). Vor allem aber bleibt Fassbinder den vom epischen Theater Brechts entlehnten und im folgenden Kapitel zu behandelnden Verfremdungstechniken treu, mit denen er bereits im „antitheater" und bei den ersten Filmproduktionen experimentiert hatte.

3.2 Ali und Emmi als „Außenseiter-Protagonisten"

Bereits durch seine Rolle als einfacher Gastarbeiter aus einem arabischen Herkunftsland wird Ali zum gesellschaftlichen Außenseiter, dessen Integration im Rahmen wachsender Fremdenfeindlichkeit nur sehr bedingt möglich ist. Als Ausländer, der eine sehr viel ältere deutsche Frau heiratet, bricht er dann gleich zwei in den siebzigerer Jahren noch sehr feste, grundsätzlich aber bis heute weiterbestehende soziale Normen. Sowohl „die Liebe und Heirat eines Paares, bei dem die Frau erheblich älter ist als der Mann" als auch „die Heirat einer deutschen Frau mit einem Ausländer" werden überwiegend als „widernatürlich" empfunden, und mit der Bereitschaft, eine solche Beziehung einzugehen, wird auch Emmi zum Außenseiter (Baier, 1975, S.8). Bis dahin lag sie als Putzfrau und alte Frau zwar am unteren Ende einer von kapitalorientierten pseudorationalistischen Normen gebildeten Werteskala, hatte aber doch einen gewissen Rückhalt in den ritualhaft, fast fassadengleich miteinander kommunizierenden Sozialgruppen ihrer Arbeitskollegen und Familie.

Ganz nach Elsaessers Charakterisierung des „Außenseiter-Protagonisten" im Neuen Deutschen Film (1994, S.283ff) ist das Hauptproblem der beiden ungleichen Personen die soziale Isolation. Der Film fokalisiert die Abwehrreaktionen der Emmi umgebenden deutschen Sozialgruppe. Hierzu gehören Grundsatzaussagen von Emmis Arbeitskollegen wie „Wer sich mit einem Ausländer einläßt, ist eine Hure", direkte Kommentare von Emmis Kindern wie „Das hättest du uns nicht antun sollen. Diese Schande", die Weigerung des Kaufmanns, Ali zu bedienen, und erste primitive Gewaltreaktionen, wie das Eintreten von Emmis Fernseher durch einen der Söhne. Aber auch die Ali umgebende ausländische Sozialgruppe reagiert mit Distanz. „Das ist unnatürlich", formuliert die an Ali interessierte namenlose Frau an der Theke.

Beiden Gruppen ist als erste Reaktion und als dauerhafte Verhaltensweise ein verständnisloses distanziertes Starren auf das ungleiche Paar gemeinsam. Emmi wird sofort zu Beginn des Films mit diesem Starren konfrontiert, als sie die Ausländerkneipe betritt. Im Wechsel fokalisiert die Kamera mehrmals Emmi bei ihrem Verhalten (Betreten des Lokals, Setzen, Bestellen) und dann jeweils das Starren der Gäste mitsamt der Besitzerin der Wirtschaft. Ali wird sehr ähnlich mit einem Starren von Emmis Kindern konfrontiert, als er ihnen in seiner neuen Rolle als Ehemann vorgestellt wird. Auch die Nachbarinnen, die Arbeitskolleginnen und der Lebensmittelhändler blicken immer wieder sehr ähnlich auf das Fremde, Ungewohnte, scheinbar Unnatürliche. Der „*act of vision*" wird so zu einem zentralen Problem und Leitsymbol für Ausgrenzung und Isolation des Liebespaares. Mayne (1977, S.72–3) umreißt die Charakteristik der Blicke: „*The individual and total effect of these looks conveys a reduction of human beings to the status of spectacle, objects existing solely for the viewer.*" Diese Objektivierung in der Perspektive der sozialen Umgebung wird durch eine häufige Einrahmung der Außenseiter verstärkt, die beim Hochzeitsmahl in Hitlers ehemaliger Gastwirtschaft besonders deutlich ist. Das ungleiche Paar sitzt hier allein an einem großen Tisch im hinteren Raum des Lokals, die Kamera bleibt aber im Vorderraum und filmt durch den Durchgang, wobei der von der Trennwand gebildete Rahmen die Sicht auf das sitzende Paar verkürzt. Die Begrenzung des Raums wird wie schon das oben umrissene Starren durch eine Zeitdehnung akzentuiert. Freilich ist es hier nur noch der Rezipient, der einige Sekunden lang auf das unbeweglich verharrende Paar starrt und so zur Auseinandersetzung mit der ausgrenzenden Umwelt gezwungen wird, deren Rolle er einnimmt. Gerade die Einrahmung ist ein sehr häufig verwendetes Mittel, um auf die Begrenzung der äußeren Perspektive aufmerksam zu machen. Wie in einem „Guckkastenraum" (Wiegand, 1974, S.33) werden die Außenseiter beim Kennenlernen in Emmis Küche durch den Türrahmen präsentiert, ähnlich dann auch Ali allein, als er mit der Besitzerin der Ausländerkneipe fremdgeht. Letzteres ist charakteristisch für das Umkehrspiel bei Fassbinder, der entgegen traditioneller Vorstellungen anstelle der Frau häufig den Mann als Objekt sexueller Begierde thematisiert. Im Falle des Gastarbeiters widerspricht diese Darstellung diametral dem von den Putzfrauen enthüllten Klischee des Frauen nur als Sexobjekt mißbrauchenden animalischen Ausländers („Die wollen nicht sprechen."), das auf die mit Ausländern zusammenlebenden Frauen zurückreflektiert wird („Die wollen nur das eine."). Die Artifizialität dieses Klischees wird deutlich, als die Putzfrauen selber in Emmis Wohnzimmer Alis Statur und Muskeln bewundern und so ihre abfälligen Kommentare als Ausdruck von Sexualneid enthüllen. Gleichzeitig verweist die Szene auf die eigentliche Gefahr für das von Ali und Emmi bis dahin mühsam erkämpfte private Glück. Beim permanenten inneren Kampf des Außenseiterprotagonisten zwischen „Rebellion und Unterordnung" (Elsaesser, 1994, S.288) liegt diese Gefahr weniger in der Rebellion gegenüber einer inhumanen sozialen Norm als in der Internalisierung derselben. Emmi fördert in dieser Szene durch Vorführung von Muskeln und Statur die Objektivierung ihres Mannes und provoziert damit seine Flucht in die Arme Barbaras. Emmi „versagt" – und dies ist ein weiteres Charakteristikum des „Außenseiter-protagonisten" im Neuen Deutschen Film (Elsaesser, 1994, S.300) – bei dem Versuch, eine harmonische Synthese zwischen sozialer Norm und dem durch die Beziehung mit Ali hergestellten Bruch dieser Norm zu konstruieren. Dies ist jedoch kaum mehr als eine „heroische Anstrengung [...] in einer höhnisch nutzlosen Situation" (Elsaesser, 1994, S.300). Alis und Emmis Versuch einer gemeinsamen Identitätsfindung widerspricht eklatant der identitätsfeindlichen objektivierenden sozialen Norm. Ein Ausgleich kann nur geschaffen werden, indem das Kollektiv zumindestens oberflächlich auf eine Sanktionierung des Normenbruchs verzichtet. Der Film zeigt, daß dies nicht utopisch ist: Nach dem Urlaub des ungleichen Paars, der vor allem den deutschen Sozialgruppen Zeit zur Reflektion gegeben hat, wird das isolierende Verhalten aufgehoben und ein Zustand der Kommunikation wiederhergestellt, der intensiver ist als der Austausch vor der Heirat der beiden Protagonisten. Daß die Motivation für diesen Verhaltensumbruch ausschließlich im jeweiligen Eigennutz der sozialen Partner zu suchen ist, entspricht „der grundsätzlichen Struktur der Interaktion der Figuren", mit der Fassbinder einen realhistorischen „Sadomasochismus" im sozialen Verhalten zu reflektieren versucht (Elsaesser, 1994, S.306). Die Ausbeutung anderer als Objekt zur Befriedigung eigener Begierden und die oft nur allzu schnelle Bereitschaft der Außenseiter zur Unterordnung bis hin zur Selbstaufgabe ist ein Thema, das in Fassbinders Filmen immer wiederkehrt und sowohl Emmis Verhalten in der skizzierten Szene als auch Alis bereitwillige Akzeptanz aller Erniedrigungen bis hin zum Ausbruch seines Magengeschwürs treffend charakterisiert. Nicht zufällig resümiert Ali im Gespräch mit Emmi das Verhältnis Deutscher – Gastarbeiter im Film zunächst prägnant mit der Formulierung „Deutscher Herr – Araber Hund" und akzeptiert dieses unmenschliche Schema später mit den Worten: „Vielleicht Deutsche haben Recht,

Arabisch nix Mensch". Der Grund für die bereitwillige Akzeptanz der eigenen Objektivierung ist in einer mehrdimensionalen Angst zu suchen, die der Arzt im Hospital bei Alis Anblick als einen für Gastarbeiter typischen „Streß" diagnostiziert. Dieser „Streß" wird durch einen Komplex von „Forderungen auf Verhalten" [25] aber auch auf äußere Aspekte provoziert, die nicht einlösbar sind. Der Lebensmittelhändler verlangt perfekte Deutschkenntnisse, der Vorarbeiter immer absolute Pünktlichkeit, die Nachbarinnen und Arbeitskollegen Emmis ein deutsches Aussehen und parallel die namenlose Ausländerin in der Asphaltbar eine permanente sexuelle Bereitschaft und Potenz. Ali hat große Angst vor der „Gemeinheit" des Vorarbeiters und bemüht sich sehr um Pünktlichkeit, auch hilft er der ihn lange Zeit diskriminierenden Frau Kargus beim Möbeltransport, der Normenkomplex bleibt freilich unerfüllbar. So bleiben Ängste wie die vor einem persönlichen Versagen, vor sozialer Ächtung, vor einer unverständlichen und unmenschlichen Gesellschaft und letztlich vor der eigenen Identität zumindestens im Unterbewußtsein allgegenwärtig. Dies gilt insbesondere für Emmi, die im Gegensatz zu Ali an eine soziale Isolation von ihrer unmittelbaren Lebenswelt sowie an „das Gaffen" anderer nicht gewöhnt ist und der Feindlichkeit offen begegnet. [26] Der an die Objektivierung gewöhnte und weitgehend fatalistische Ali enthüllt seine Ängste mehr über das Verständnis von Emmis Ängsten und über den plötzlichen Ausbruch seines Magengeschwürs.

Durch eine tableauartige Anordnung werden auch die auf Ali und Emmi starrenden Personen objektiviert. Gleich zu Beginn des Films erscheinen die beim Anblick Emmis regungslos verharrenden Gäste der Ausländerkneipe in ihrer über mehrere Kameraeinstellungen hinweg unveränderten Zusammenstellung am Ende der Theke als artifizielle Gruppe. Ähnlich künstlich wirken auch die auf Ali und Emmi starrenden Bediensteten eines Gartenlokals. Der wiederholte Einstellungswechsel vom ungleichen Liebespaar, das als einziger Gast genau in der Mitte zahlloser leerer Tische Platz bezogen hat, zu der – wie für eine Aufnahme

---

25 Vgl. Hegenbarth-Rösgen (1982, S.17f.) zur Definition von „sozialer Norm".
26 Hierzu gehört das zur Rede stellen des Lebensmittelhändlers („Warum bedienen Sie meinen Mann nicht?"), der Versuch einer offenen Aussprache mit den Arbeitskollegen („Warum seid ihr so komisch? ... Seid doch nicht so, gebt mir ein Messer.") und vor allem der Wutausbruch im Gartenlokal („Warum gafft ihr so? ... Das ist mein Mann, ihr Schweine.").

zusammengestellten und unbeweglich bleibenden – Bedienstetengruppe macht die Starrenden selber zum Objekt der Betrachtung.

Beide Formen der Objektivierung zwingen den Rezipienten ganz nach Brechts Ausführungen zur Verfremdung im epischen Theater (Brecht, 1994, S.25–55), die Fassbinder bereits von seiner Arbeit beim Action Theater und beim „antitheater" kannte (Gemünden, 1994, S.60–1), zu einer kognitiven Auseinandersetzung mit dem kollektiven Verhalten. Vor allem die tableauartige Präsentation der gesellschaftlichen Gruppen und die Einrahmung der Außenseiter folgen der Kernforderung des Brechtschen Anti-Illusionismus, daß „der wirkliche, profane Vorgang [d.h. der Schauspielcharakter des Gezeigten] nicht mehr verschleiert" werden darf. Bei aller notwendigen Nähe zum Vertrauten, welche die Transferierbarkeit des Gezeigten in den Erfahrungshorizont des Rezipienten sicherstellt, gilt es doch, die Illusion zu zerstören, „der Schauspieler sei die Figur, und die Vorführung sei das Geschehnis". Erst die „Verfremdung des Vertrauten" ermöglicht, die Zweifelhaftigkeit und Abänderbarkeit dieses Vertrauten zu enthüllen. Im Mittelpunkt der Darstellung hat daher ein „Akt des Zeigens" zu stehen, der „die gesellschaftlichen Zustände als Prozesse" entlarvt und „in ihrer Widersprüchlichkeit" verfolgt (Brecht, 1994, S.40ff). Immer wieder präsentiert Fassbinder so Hindernisse, die den Blick des Rezipienten stören und mit der filmischen Illusion brechen. In auffällig paralleler Einstellung werden Emmi und die jugoslawische Gastarbeiterin Jolanda hinter dem Treppengeländer wie hinter Gittern sitzend präsentiert, was auf deren Gefangenschaft in einem Netz von sozialen Normen und Vorurteilen hinweist. Emmis Nachbarin, Frau Kargus, erscheint wiederholt hinter einem zum Treppenhaus ragenden Fenster, dessen Gitter allerdings mehr an die eines Beichtstuhls erinnern. Dies entspricht Frau Kargus eigener Auffassung von ihrer Stellung als „ *moral custodian of the building and, in particular, as ‚mother confessor' to Emmi's sexual sinner*" (Burns, 1995, S.68). Die echte Beichte, in der Emmi fast monologartig Ali gegenüber ihre Einsamkeit eingesteht, erfolgt freilich viel früher. Hier benutzt Fassbinder eine in Sirks *All that heaven allows* modellhaft vorgeführte Nahaufnahme der erzählenden Person, bei der die angesprochene Person betont unscharf im Hintergrund zu erkennen bleibt. Die Vielfältigkeit der visuellen Verfremdungstechniken ist freilich in *Angst essen Seele auf* ungleich größer. Exemplarisch integriert Fassbinder die in *All that heaven allows* zentrale Stadt-Land-Antithese in sehr stilisierter Form. Während im Sirkschen Melodrama Rons Naturbezogenheit eine direkte Verbindung zum Land als idealerem Lebensraum herstellt, wird diese Opposition in Fassbinders Film über eine auffällige Häufung ruraler bzw. exotistisch-naturbezogener Bilder in Emmis Wohnung, in der Asphaltbar und im italienischen Restaurant eingeblendet. Die Beschränkung auf Abbildungen verdeutlicht, daß für Ali und Emmi kein Rückzug ins private Idyll möglich ist (vgl. hierzu Burns, 1995, S.60).

Verfremdungen zeigen sich auch bei der Sprache. So ist auffällig, daß der vom Lebensmittelhändler wegen seiner mangelnden Deutschkenntnisse nicht bediente, bzw. wegen einem Normenverstoß sanktionierte Ali emotional komplexe Situationen sehr viel besser erfassen und ausdrücken kann als seine deutsche Umgebung. Nicht nur erfaßt er mit der Formulierung „Angst essen Seele auf" seine und Emmis Situation prägnant, er vermag auch über die betont freundlich-offene Formulierung eines einfachen „Guten Tag" Emmis Bedenken zu der fremden neuen Beziehung zu zerstreuen (Burns, 1995, S.66). Demgegenüber zeigt sich die sprachliche Hilflosigkeit der deutschen Umgebung sehr deutlich, als einer von Emmis Söhnen vor lauter Wut über den Gastarbeiter in der Familie wortlos den Fernseher seiner Mutter eintritt. Aber auch in der von Fassbinder selber (als Eugen) und von Irm Hermann (als Krista) gespielten typischen neu-kleinbürgerlichen deutschen Zweierfamilie dominiert die Inkommunikation. Unterhaltungen beschränken sich im Wesentlichen auf Befehle („Bring mir das Bier."), auf Vorwürfe („Du bist nur zu faul.") und auf den bereits im Ansatz scheiternden Versuch einer Verschleierung der privaten Misere („Benimm dich wenigstens, wenn Mutter da ist."). Vor diesem Hintergrund ist der selbst im Filmtitel akzentuierte Infinitivstil Alis weniger als Ausdruck sprachlicher Hilflo-sigkeit von Gastarbeitern denn als „aggressive Karikatur einer trivialen öffentlichen Perspektive" gegenüber den Immigranten [27] zu verstehen.

Erst die Menge und Vielfältigkeit visueller und sprachlicher

---

[27] Vgl. Freybourg (1993, S.74) zur Karikatur von Sprachklischees.

Verfremdungen führt den Rezipienten zu einer deutlichen Distanzierung vom Geschehen. Die emotionale Identifikation mit den Charakteren wird schon durch deren Selbstreflektion vor Spiegeln begrenzt. Emmi etwa läuft fast panisch zum Badezimmerspiegel, nachdem sie mit Ali zum ersten Mal geschlafen hat, und drückt so ihre Angst vor den Folgen des Normenbruchs aus. Ali betrachtet sich nach einer Phase des Fremdgehens, der Trinkerei und Spielerei in einem Toilettenspiegel der Asphaltbar und beginnt sich selber zu ohrfeigen (vgl Burns, 1995, S.63). Diese Distanzierung aber mündet in Lowrys Resümee (1984, S.30), daß Fassbinder hier einen Film produziert hat *„ which will make audiences both think and feel"*. Eine Synthese zwischen dem publikumswirksamen, emotional sehr ansprechenden Sirkschen Melodrama und der stilisierten Verfremdung eines Bertolt Brecht gefunden zu haben, ist denn auch als die zentrale Leistung Fassbinders bei *Angst essen Seele auf* hervorzuheben. Nur aus der Einsicht dieser Leistung erklärt sich die fast arrogante Selbstabhebung Fassbinders, Brecht sei jemand *„ who makes the audience think. I make the audience feel and think"* (Gemünden, 1994, S.59).

3.3 Ansätze zur Lösung der Außenseiterproblematik im Film

Das Ende des Films läßt Raum für die Hoffnung auf ein glückliches Ende der Zweierbeziehung, aber auch für eine pessimistische Deutung. Eine gewisse Aussöhnung mit der Umwelt ist erreicht, und Emmi und Ali sind wieder vereint, aber das vom „Streß" auf die Gastarbeiter entstandene Magengeschwür Alis soll nach Erfahrung des Arztes immer wieder ausbrechen. Emmi kontert zwar mit der Bemerkung, daß dies nicht der Fall sein wird, wenn sie sich Mühe gibt, es bleibt jedoch offen, inwieweit eine psychosomatisch auf die Allgegenwärtigkeit unmenschlicher Normen zurückzuführende Krankheit auf privater Ebene erfolgreich bekämpft werden kann. Der Film hat zunächst eine weitgehende individuelle Machtlosigkeit der Außenseiter und damit ein weiteres Charakteristikum des Außenseiterprotagonisten im Neuen Deutschen Film (vgl. Elsaesser, 1994, S.290) gezeigt. Weder Alis fatalistische Akzeptanz von Normen und daran entwickelten Vorurteilen noch Emmis offene Opposition konnten die Isolation aufbrechen. Vielmehr sind die Außenseiter durch Befolgung einer zentralen Norm, nämlich der Institutionalisierung ihrer Beziehung durch Heirat, in die absolute

Marginalisierung gedrängt worden. Die Akzeptanz und aktive Förderung von Alis Objektivierung hat sich als selbstzerstörerisch enthüllt.

So bleibt nur die Hoffnung auf eine dauerhafte Verhaltensänderung der Umgebung, die allerdings von den Außenseitern durch eine konsequente und vor allem gemeinsame Abkehr von dieser Umgebung gefördert werden kann. Auf die Ablehnung ihres Ehemannes durch den Lebensmittelhändler reagiert Emmi mit dem Boykott des kleinen Lebensmittelhandels, auf die Abkehr von Familie und Arbeitskollegen mit einer Flucht in das private Glück, das eine Urlaubsreise zu zweit zu versprechen vermag. Diese einfache Form der Auflehnung hat Erfolg, weil der Eigennutz die Gesellschaft zu einer erneuten Annäherung treibt. So bleibt ein Zusammenschluß der Außenseiter eine zentrale Forderung, die *Angst essen Seele auf* exemplarisch für den Neuen Deutschen Film zur Lösung der Außenseiterproblematik aufstellt. Hier ist das von Sanders (1985, S.136) hervorgehobene Zahlenverhältnis zwischen den vom Neuen Deutschen Kino häufig fokalisierten unterdrückten Sozialgruppen, „Gastarbeiter, *old people and women*‘, und der Restgesellschaft von besonderer Bedeutung. Allein diese „Außenseiter" sind mit einem Zwei-Drittel-Anteil an der Gesamtbevölkerung in der absoluten Majorität. Sie müssen sich dieser gemeinsamen Rolle „nur" bewußt werden und durch eine gemeinsame klare Abkehr von der sie marginalisierenden Gesellschaft wehren. Die von Fassbinder als „masochistisch" empfundene Tendenz zur selbstzerstörerischen Unterordnung ist freilich groß und auch in *Angst essen Seele auf* keineswegs aufgehoben.

Hilfe von einer Regierung zu erwarten, wäre sinnentleert. Die im Film skizzierten Formen der Diskriminierung sind mit gesetzlichen Maßnahmen kaum effektiv zu bekämpfen. [28] Vor allem aber geht der offizielle Diskurs im Entstehungszeitraum von Fassbinders Film sowohl mit den Anwerbeversprechen als auch mit der Berichterstattung über den massiven Zuzug von Türken in einigen deutschen Städten, vollständig an der individuellen menschlichen Dimension der

---

28 Vgl. Funcke (1987, S.25): „Alles, was Parlamente und Regierungen tun können, sind Regelungen formaler, rechtlicher und administrativer Art. Wirkliche Integration kann nur von Mensch zu Mensch erreicht werden, in der Herstellung von Bezügen, in gegenseitigem Verständnis, in unmittelbarer Begegnung."

Außenseiterproblematik vorbei, bei der die Gastarbeiter nur ein zahlenmäßig relativ kleines Beispiel für die Marginalisierung der meisten Menschen in einer nach kapitalorientierten pseudorationalen Grundsätzen strukturierten modernen Industrienation sind.

4 Schlußwort

Wenn Sanders (1985, S.136) als unterdrückte Sozialgruppen und damit Protagonisten des Neuen Deutschen Films „Gastarbeiter, *old people and women*" hervorhebt, so ist Fassbinders *Angst essen Seele auf* zumindestens in thematischer Hinsicht das Exemplum schlechthin. Über den Gastarbeiter Ali und die alte Putzfrau Emmi stellt der Film – wenngleich bei klarem Fokus auf die „eigentliche Gastarbeiter- problematik" – gleich alle drei Gruppen in den Vordergrund. So verwundert auch nicht, daß die von Elsässer (1994, S.283ff.) für die „Außenseiter-Protagonisten" des Neuen Deutschen Films erarbeiteten Kategorien Isolation, existenzielle Angst, innerer Kampf zwischen Rebellion und Unterordnung, persönliche Machtlosigkeit und Versagen auf Ali und Emmi gleichermaßen anwendbar sind. Fassbinder geht es sicher insbesondere aber nicht nur um die Marginalisierung von Gastarbeitern. Diese sind vielmehr Beispiel für das Außenseitertum einer absoluten Mehrheit von Menschen in einer von inhumanen pseudorationalen Normen bestimmten Gesellschaft. Die in der modernistischen Literatur immer wieder thematisierte Identitäts- problematik des modernen Menschen ist mit ähnlichen Attributen wie etwa bei Brecht, Kafka und Sábato auch bei Godard und Fassbinder wiederzufinden. Die Vorstellung von einer Objektivierung des Menschen wird in *Angst essen Seele auf* nicht zufällig streng nach Brechts Ausführungen zur Verfremdungstechnik (vgl. Burns, 1995; Gemünden, 1994) reaktualisiert. Wenn die von Ali und Emmi inmitten ihrer Lebenswelt erfahrene Isolation und Inkommunikation auch nicht so absolut ist wie die des Handelsreisenden in Kafkas *Verwandlung* (1915) oder die des Malers Juan Pablo Castel in Sábatos *El túnel* (1948), ein dauerhaftes existenzielles Problem ist sie schon, und eine Patentlösung ist auch bei Fassbinder nicht in Sicht. Freilich bleibt in *Angst essen Seele auf* zumindestens die vage Hoffnung, daß die auf Eigennutz aufgebaute Gesellschaft durch einen dauerhaften

Zusammenschluß der Außenseiter zu einer Relativierung der eigenen Normen gezwungen werden kann und so ein annähernd menschliches Leben theoretisch möglich ist. Fassbinder weist im Gegensatz zu Kafka und Sábato einen zwar nicht unproblematischen, aber doch wenigstens vorstellbaren Weg, und dieser sollte auch beim Unterrichtseinsatz seines Films vermittelt werden.

Literaturliste

Albaladejo Y Fuertes J, *Migration und Vorurteil. Abneigung gegen ausländische Arbeitnehmer in der BRD* (Aachen, unveröffentlichte Dissertation, 1987)

Baier E, 'Angst essen Seele auf' in: *Filmbesprechungen,* Bd. 22, S.7–10 (1975)

Berling S, *Die 13 Jahre des Rainer Werner Fassbinder. Seine Filme, seine Freunde, seine Feinde* (Bergisch Gladbach, Gustav Lübbe Verlag, 1992)

Brecht B, 'Kleines Organon für das Theater' in: *Theaterarbeit* (Frankfurt am Main, Suhrkamp, 1994)

Bundesministerium (Hg.) *Betrifft: Ausländerpolitik.* (Bonn, Universitäts-Buchdruckerei, 1983)

Burns R, 'Fassbinder's *Angst essen Seele auf.* A mellow Brechtian drama' in: *German Life and Letters,* Bd. 48, S.56–74 (1995)

Corrigan T, *New German Film. The displaced image* (Bloomington, Indianapolis, Indiana University Press, 1994)

Elsaesser T, 'Tales of sound and fury: Observations of the family melodrama' in: *Monogram,* Bd. 4, S.2–15, (1972)

―――. *Der Neue Deutsche Film. Von den Anfängen bis zu den neunziger Jahren* (München, Wilhelm Heyne Verlag, 1994)

Faltin I, *Norm – Milieu – politische Kultur: normative Vernetzungen in Gesellschaft und Politik der Bundesrepublik* (Wiesbaden, Deutscher Universitäts Verlag, 1990)

Feldmann S, 'Der Motor des deutschen Films' in: *Rheinische Post* (12.6.1982)

Fischer R, and Hembus J, *Der Neue Deutsche Film 1960–1980* (München, Goldmann Verlag, 1981)

Freybourg A M, *Film und Autor. Eine Analyse des Autorenkinos von Jean-Luc Godard und Rainer Werner Fassbinder* (Hamburg, unveröffentlichte Dissertation, 1993)

Funcke L, 'Von "Gastarbeitern" zu sprachlichen und kulturellen Minderheiten' in: Bundeszentrale für Politische Bildung (Hg.): *Ausländer und Massenmedien. Bestandsaufnahme und Perspektiven* (Bonn: Bundeszentrale, S.23–26, 1987)

Gemünden G, 'Re-fusing Brecht: The cultural politics of Fassbinder's German Hollywood' in: *New German Critique* (Bd. 63, S.55–76, 1994)

Hauptman I, 'Defending melodrama' in: *Themes in Drama* (Bd. 14, S.281–289, 1992)

Hegenbarth-Rösgen A, *Soziale Normen und Rollen im Roman* (München, Wilhelm Fink Verlag, 1982)

Henrichs B, 'Müder Wunderknabe. Rainer Werner Fassbinder: Von der Theaterkommune zur Kunstfabrik' in: *Zeitmagazin* (8.6.1973)

Herrmann H, 'Ursachen und Entwicklung der Ausländerbeschäftigung' in: *Informationen zur politischen Bildung* (237, S.4–5, 1992)

Impressum (Hg.) *Materialien zum Keller-Kino. Rainer Werner Fassbinder* (Hildesheim, Impressum, 1977)

Kim (Hg.) (1974) *film-dienst* (Köln, Institutsverlag)

———. *Lexikon des Internationalen Films* (Hamburg, Rowohlt, 1987)

———. *Caligaris Erben. Der Katalog zum Thema 'Psychatrie im Film'* (Bonn, Psychatrie-Verlag, 1994)

Kistler, H (Hg.) *Die Bundesrepublik Deutschland. Vorgeschichte und Geschichte 1945–1983* (Stuttgart, Verlag Bonn Aktuell, 1983)

Klöpper M (Hg.) *Ausländerfeindlichkeit in der BRD.* (Oldenburg, Bibliotheks- und Informationssystem der Universität Oldenburg, 1985)

Krusche D (Hg.) *Reclams Filmführer* (Stuttgart, Philipp Reclam jun. 1991)

Limmer W, *Rainer Werner Fassbinder, Filmemacher* (Hamburg, Rowohlt, 1981)

Lorenz J (ed.), *Das ganz normale Chaos. Gespräche über Rainer Werner Fassbinder* (Berlin, Henschel Verlag, 1995)

Lowry E, 'Angst essen Seele auf' (Rez.) in: Lyon C (Hg.): *The Macmillan dictionary of films and filmmakers.* Bd. I: *Films* (London, Macmillan, S.29–30, 1984)

Märthesheimer P, 'Das forschende Kind. Einige Steine des Hauses, das Rainer Werner Fassbinder zu bauen begonnen hatte' in: Pflaum, H G, (Hg.) *Jahrbuch Film 82/83. Berichte, Kritiken, Daten* (München, Wien: Carl Hanser Verlag, 1982)

Mayne J, 'Fassbinder and spectatorship' in: *New German Critique,* Bd. 12, S.61–74 (1977)

Müller K B, 'Die unendliche Geschichte der Einsamkeit. Rainer Werner Fassbinder 1945–1982' *Kulturchronik* (Bd. 2, S.21–23, 1992)

Nash, J R and Ross, S (eds.) *The motion picture guide* (Chicago, Cinebooks, 1986)

Ney, H-G 'Was deutsche Volksschüler über ausländische Arbeiter denken' in: Klee E (Hg.), *Gastarbeiter. Analysen und Berichte* (Frankfurt am Main, Suhrkamp, 1975)

———. *Film in der Bundesrepublik Deutschland* (München, Wien, Carl Hanser Verlag, 1979)

Pflaum H G, *Rainer Werner Fassbinder. Bilder und Dokumente* (München, Edition Spangenberg, 1992)

Rentschler E, (Hg.) *West German filmmakers on film: Visions and voices* (New York, London, Homes & Meier, 1988)

Roud R, (ed.) *Cinema. A critical dictionary. The major film-makers* (London, Secker & Warburg, 1980)

Sandford J, *The New German Cinema* (New York, Da Capo Press, 1985)

Schöneberg U, 'Gruppenpsychologische Hintergründe der Fremdenangst und Fremdenfeindlichkeit' in: Bundeszentrale für politische Bildung (Hg.): *Ausländer und Massenmedien. Bestandsaufnahme und Perspektiven* (Bonn, Bundeszentrale, S.36–57, 1987)

Schütte W, 'Das Herz. Die künstlerische physiognomie Rainer Werner Fassbinders im Augenblick seines Verlustes' in: *Frankfurter Rundschau* (19.6.1982)

————. 'Unser Balzac ist tot. Rainer Werner Fassbinder 1946–1982' in: *Kulturchronik* (Bd. 1, S.14–16, 1983)

Sharp W, 'Structure of melodrama'. *Themes in Drama* (Bd. 14, S.269–280, 1992)

Talon G, 'Rainer Werner Fassbinder. Les respects et les craintes d'hommes-en-société' in: *Cinema* (Bd. 192, S.43–57, 1974)

Töteberg M, 'Rainer Werner Fassbinder' in: *Filme befreien den Kopf. Essays und Arbeitsnotizen* (Frankfurt am Main, Fischer Taschenbuch, 1984)

————. (Hg.) *Metzler Film Lexikon* (Stuttgart, Weimar, Metzler, 1995)

Wiegand W, 'Die Puppe in der Puppe. Beobachtungen zu Fassbinders Filmen' in: Jansen P W and W Schütte (Hg.): *Rainer Werner Fassbinder* (5. Auflage, Frankfurt am Main, Fischer Taschenbuch, 1992)

80

5 | What is German cinema? Approaches to popular film

Erica Carter
University of Warwick

1 Introduction

In the undergraduate film course that I have taught now for a number of years, I regularly begin with a straw poll to establish what, if anything, students already know of German cinema. From year to year, responses are remarkably similar. Students who have knowingly encountered contemporary German films will have done so in the context of 'A' level courses where they have looked at this or that example of New German Cinema: *Die verlorene Ehre der Katharina Blum* (Schlöndorff and von Trotta, 1975) is an old chestnut, or sometimes Fassbinder's *Angst essen Seele auf* (1973), the latter viewed usually in the context of project work on multiculturalism and migrant labour. The smattering of film buffs in the group may have attended a rare art house showing of Robert Wiene's 1919 classic *Das Cabinet des Dr Caligari* or Murnau's *Nosferatu – Eine Symphonie des Grauens* (1921/2) – though those prepared to choose these in preference to the latest Hollywood action blockbuster are few and far between. Finally, my classroom survey may turn up the occasional historical enthusiast whose interest in fascism has led to an acquaintance with the Leni Riefenstahl oeuvre – and often to an unfortunate perception of *Triumph des Willens* (1935) as the first and last word in German cinema.

Weimar Expressionism, Nazi propaganda, the seventies and eighties classics of New German Cinema: such have traditionally been the contours of 'German cinema' as conceived in German Studies curricula from secondary level on. This selective focus, one could of course argue, merely reflects the moments at which German cinema made its most significant international impact. Thus for instance Weimar Expressionism was internationally lauded from its inception as heralding a new era in the development of the film medium itself. Siegfried Kracauer notes, for example, how European observers of the time admired German talent in the 'whole visual sphere' (Kracauer, 1947, p.3). Particularly celebrated were German skill in *mise-en-scène*, especially setting and lighting, as well as the fluidity of the mobile camera pioneered by Murnau, for example, most notably in his collaboration with the virtuoso cameraman Karl Freund in *Der letzte Mann* (1924). Nazi propaganda film, of course, achieved a different kind of international fame – or better, notoriety – when it drew on the same talent in the construction of visual spectacle to produce what appeared the most sophisticated propaganda apparatus yet seen in the international film industry. New German Cinema, conversely, was internationally hailed as a return of a different kind to the glories of Weimar. Here was an art cinema that easily measured up to the aesthetic achievements of its nineteen-twenties precursor, while avoiding the political traps of a German film culture which many claimed had remained ideologically tainted long after the collapse of the Third Reich in 1945.

But the canonical status in German Film Studies of a small handful of films from these three periods is not attributable solely to their critical reception at the time of their release. It is the result also of historiographical procedures that, at any given moment, bring into focus a particular and limited selection of films, while consigning others to a status as mere background – a set of footnotes to a larger film history. In each of our three exemplary periods – Weimar, Nazism and New German Cinema – historical analysis has conventionally been framed by one of two core assumptions. In the first instance, German cinema has been construed first and foremost as high cultural art cinema. Not only is Germany seen to have provided world cinema with some of its most influential *auteurs*, from F.W. Murnau and Fritz Lang, to Rainer Werner Fassbinder, Werner Herzog and Wim Wenders. More than this, German film is represented as crucial to broader aesthetic developments in cinematic modernism, most centrally through the expressionist experiments of the Weimar years, but more recently too in the studied rejection of Hollywood realism that characterises much of the body of work we know as the New German Cinema.

The second assumption traditionally underpinning historical studies of German film (an assumption rather opposed to the first, with its emphasis on aesthetic issues) is what Thomas Elsaesser has termed the *Sonderweg* hypothesis in the cinematic realm: the assumption, that is, that Germany's 'separate development into modernity' (Elsaesser 1996, p.11), and specifically, the social, political and humanitarian catastrophe that was National Socialism, demands that all modern Germany's cultural products be judged primarily as political and ideological phenomena. Siegfried Kracauer's *From Caligari to Hitler. A psychological history of the German film* (1947), one of the two founding studies of Weimar cinema (the other is Lotte Eisner's *The haunted screen,* first published in French in 1955), sets the tone when it claims to identify in Weimar film culture a proto-fascist obsession with authoritarian rule. As Kracauer himself puts the argument, 'behind the overt history of economic shifts, social exigencies and political machinations runs a secret history involving the inner dispositions of the German people. The disclosure of these dispositions through the medium of the German screen may help in the understanding of Hitler's ascent and ascendancy' (p.11).

Kracauer's method in *From Caligari to Hitler* is to reconstruct, largely through plot analysis, the cinematic traces of mass political anxieties and collective desires. Thus in his account the Expressionist classics become, not aesthetic models from a golden age of artistic innovation, but studies in a collective German fantasy of totalitarian domination. *Das Cabinet des Dr Caligari,* for instance, the story of a fairground performer who uses autosuggestion to incite a somnambulist to murder, can best be seen, Kracauer famously argues, as representing 'an unlimited authority that idolises power as such, and, to satisfy its lust for domination, ruthlessly violates all human rights and values' (p.65). Of Murnau's *Nosferatu,* he similarly claims that the film's portrayal of a 'blood-sucking tyrant figure looming in those regions where myth and fairy tales meet,' reinforces a preoccupation with tyrannical rule that will lead the German polity ultimately to an embracing of National Socialism (p.79).

Critiques and revisions of Kracauer are many and various. Film historians have questioned his criteria of selection, claiming that the popular genre cinema Kracauer often ignored must be given at least equal social significance with the Expressionist classics (Petro, 1989; Hake, 1992). Film critics have also questioned Kracauer's method of retrospective interpretation – his tendency to read fascism backwards into texts from the late teens and early twenties. But more interesting for our purposes here than individual revisitings and reworkings of Kracauer is a much broader paradigm shift, a shift in models of film historiography that, amongst other things, may profoundly change the ways we conceive of this or that film as an appropriate object of analysis for German Film Studies in the classroom.

2 German cinema and the new film history

To illustrate that change, let us look again at the case of Weimar cinema. Weimar film history has as its founding texts two critical works that reproduce the two paradigmatic assumptions of German film history in general: the definition of German cinema either as art cinema *tout court*, or as a vehicle for socio-political expression. While Lotte Eisner's *The haunted screen* identifies aspects of film form, especially visual style, as the proper focus of critical attention, Kracauer's *From Caligari to Hitler* paints a picture of Weimar film as a mirror to the political unconscious of the German nation. Despite their differences, however, Eisner and Kracauer share a common view of the relation between the film texts they analyse, and the socio-political context that engendered them. Thus just as, for Kracauer, the films he discussed 'reflect (German) mentality in a more direct way than other artistic media' (p.5), so too for Eisner, 1920s Expressionist style reproduced 'innate German longings' (p.21) for stark contrasts and mysterious shadows.

Such accounts of the film text's essentially mimetic relation to the national psyche or national history began, however, increasingly to conflict with film theory and film criticism as it developed from the 1970s on. From the early 1970s, academic Film Studies in Britain and the US in particular began to search for an approach to film that would avoid the reflection hypothesis of previous accounts, while at the same time continuing to situate film within larger socio-political and cultural histories. It was in this context that attention began increasingly to focus on what Film Studies terms 'spectatorship'. The category of the spectator, as Judith Mayne explains (1993, p.38), is on one level an historical term that refers simply to the empirical viewer of any given film. This shift in the focus of film analysis from production (the industry, the director) and text (film as art) to consumption (the film viewer) was however already of broader significance, implying as it did a fundamental rethinking of the cultural status of the film medium itself. The young discipline of Film Studies, in Britain and the United States at least, was born in the moment of the post-1968 New Left, and shared at least some of its founding assumptions regarding the political status of culture, film culture included. In the neo-Marxist analysis out of which had sprung the movements of '68 and after, developments in modern capitalism were seen to have blunted the edge of mass dissent, and cast doubt over that revolutionary future which classical Marxism had deemed inevitable. Capitalism had not produced, as nineteenth-century Marxists foresaw, the increasing impoverishment of the working-class masses and thus popular dissent, but had led instead – at least in the western world after World War II – to mass prosperity.

This was, in other words, a society in which individuals were as likely to define themselves through personal consumption – the cars they drove, the clothes they wore, or indeed, their choice of novels, magazines or films – as by their political allegiances or work identities. From this new primacy of consumption, the neo-Marxists drew conflicting conclusions. In a German context, the so-called Frankfurt School Marxists, most famously Theodor W. Adorno and Max Horkheimer in their *Dialektik der Aufklärung* (1971: first published 1947), saw mass consumerism as erasing critical opposition to contemporary capitalism; for it fostered the illusion that commodity consumption alone could realise the dreams of a better life that were once the motor of radical political organisation.

85

As is suggested by the title of their famous essay, ' *Kulturindustrie. Aufklärung als Massenbetrug*' (1971, pp.108–150), Adorno and Horkheimer saw cultural artefacts as entirely enmeshed in the industrial system that engendered them. Outside Germany, however, social philosophers seeking to comprehend the increasing complexity of modern culture turned to modes of analysis that emphasised the relative autonomy of cultural systems – their capacity to operate at a tangent from, or even occasionally in opposition to prevailing economic interests. When French cultural theory (a key influence in contemporary Film Studies) turned to structuralist semiotics and anthropology, for instance, it did so in an effort to explore how cultural systems – film, advertising, the print media – may operate according to a cultural logic that must be kept at least theoretically distinct from the market logic that first produces them. Thus while, for example, Adorno and Horkheimer condemn the very structure of Hollywood narrative for the way it echoes and reinforces the structured tedium of working lives in contemporary capitalism, semioticians might look instead for the ambivalences and tensions in narrative forms: their capacity in the first instance to expose social contradictions (every good story needs dramatic conflict), even if, in the end, those contradictions are apparently resolved in the classical Hollywood happy end.

It was this emphasis within contemporary cultural theory on the ambiguities of cultural texts – or at least, on their irreducibility to meanings determined at the point of production – that led to a new focus in cultural, literary and indeed Film Studies on the role of the cultural consumer (or 'spectator', in the case of film) as a figure with an active role to play in determining the meaning of any given text. Drawing on insights from anthropology, semiotics and psychoanalysis, the new film theory, in other words, has increasingly argued that a film's meaning is never pre-given, but is rather historically produced in a series of interactions between spectator and text.

For German film history, film theory's preoccupation with spectatorship has had important implications. Foremost amongst these is its impact on critical method. If a film's meaning is the result of historically specific interactions between text and spectator, then it follows that analysis must start, not with the search for some intrinsic textual meaning, but with an examination of the practice or process by which, in particular historical contexts, film texts gain meaning and value for given groups of spectators. And indeed, examples of revisionist histories that accord a centrality of this kind to spectatorship, are many and various. They range from psychoanalytically inspired accounts of Weimar cinema as a vehicle for social fantasy (Elsaesser, 1983, 1984, 1989), through feminist accounts of the appeal of silent cinema to female audiences of the Wilhelmine and Weimar periods (Hake, 1993; Hansen, 1990; Petro, 1989; Schlüpmann, 1990), to studies that rewrite the history of German film through a textual analysis of modes of address and spectatorial engagement (Rentschler, 1996; Silberman, 1995). These works are highly innovative as models for film history, not least in their privileging of close textual analysis over the historical overview. Thus Marc Silberman sees it as his goal in *German cinema. Texts and contexts* (1995), 'not to (re)constitute the canon of German films or to describe a tour through the imaginary museum of the German cinema', but rather to '(read) closely a selection of exemplary films...in order to conceptualise retrospectively the context in which particular meanings circulated' (p.ix).

Here, as across the range of examples cited above, the attention of the film historian has shifted away from historical overviews that assume a mimetic relation between text and context, film and history, to case study-based histories that use textual analysis to explore the dynamic between spectator and text – a dynamic that is crucial, it is argued, to the anchoring of film in its cultural context and historical moment.

3 *Wunschkonzert*: a case study

To illustrate some of the implications of this methodological shift, let us turn now to a brief case study of our own. The film I want to discuss is Eduard von Borsody's *Wunschkonzert* (1940). The title refers to the hugely popular radio programme of the same name, which, broadcast weekly as it was throughout Germany, as well as on the battlefront and to the occupied territories, provided a lifeline of communication between loved ones separated by war. The film too was amongst the most popular of its period, reaching an estimated audience on its release of over 20 million (Fuhrmann, 1992, p.14).

Film-historical references to *Wunschkonzert* have until recently focused on its propaganda status. The film tells the story of a love match between the young star Inge (Ilse Werner) and the dashing *Luftwaffe* lieutenant Herbert (Carl Raddatz). Romance is born when the couple meet in the crowd at the 1936 Berlin Olympics. The chance encounter offers the director an opportunity to recycle some stirring documentary footage of the Games; and it is this amongst other things that led early commentators to situate the film as one of Nazi cinema's most successful attempts at propagandistic entertainment. David Welch, for example, describes the film as one that 'makes capital out of the Olympic Games' by reproducing in the Olympic sequence the 'pagan exaltation of athletic prowess' that was so central to Nazi myths of racial purity (Welch, 1983, pp.120–121).

As Marc Silberman's more recent reading of *Wunschkonzert* suggests, however, an account that portrays the film, as does Welch, merely as a vehicle for pre-given ideological content, cannot adequately explain its massive popular appeal. This was a film that combined propagandistic with entertainment values in ways that were path-breaking at the time; but its impact can only properly be understood, argues Silberman, if we explore the 'visual and narrational conventions' that allow it so successfully to 'monopolise the mass public's imagination' (Silberman, 1995, p.67).

One of the characteristic stylistic features of *Wunschkonzert* is its intercutting of documentary with studio footage – a technique that lends topicality to what is otherwise a timeless narrative of unrequited love. It is from content analysis of the documentary passages that David Welch extrapolates his argument about the film's commitment to fascist ideologies of racial health. Content analysis can tell us little, however, of the relationship between overtly propagandistic sequences of this kind, and the romance narrative with which, in the film, they are intricately entwined.

The cinematic technique that establishes relations between disparate film elements is, of course, the edit. Close analysis of this aspect of film form may therefore reveal much, both about the relation *Wunschkonzert* establishes between propaganda and romance, and about the position established for an implied audience by the film's intertwining of narratives of war and romantic love. Let us look, then, at the function of editing in the scenes from the Olympic Games discussed by Welch: scenes that are intercut with a series of sequences that set in motion Inge and Herbert's romance. The first montage of actuality shots from the Olympic Games is placed immediately after the opening credits, in a sequence that directly recalls the grandiose documentary style of contemporary propaganda directors. Leni Riefenstahl especially was celebrated for the rhythmic editing, mobile camera, superimposed shots of insignia drenched with symbolic import (the Olympic symbol, tolling bells), vertiginous aerial shots and so on that we witness also in the opening shots of *Wunschkonzert.* Yet the awe which this grand beginning might inspire is mitigated by the more intimate emotions evoked by a sequence immediately following the Olympic opening. From a final aerial shot taken from actuality footage of the Olympic crowd, we cut to a long shot of a staged crowd sequence. The camera now tracks in, guiding the viewer through the crowd until we identify Inge, the main protagonist and primary focus of audience interest for the rest of the film. Inge and her aunt are framed together searching in vain for two tickets which, they now discover, have been left behind. When the aunt hails a taxi to go in search of the missing tickets, Inge waits behind, and we cut now to Herbert at the entrance to the stadium. Herbert, it transpires, has by chance a spare ticket for the event. The sequence that follows receives what seems at first the classic visual treatment of romance in narrative cinema. Herbert catches sight of Inge in the crowd: point-of-view editing places Inge, for both Herbert and the audience, as the object of an admiring gaze. His amorous interest clearly aroused, Herbert rushes to Inge's side. She stands centre-frame as he enters from frame left – an intrusive and initially unwanted presence.

German audiences of 1940 were as familiar as we are today with the conventions of classical Hollywood romance (Hollywood imports were not banned in Germany until 1939); so they would have recognised this sequence of (male) point-of-view shot followed by couple in two-shot as the conventional prelude to a happy romance. In *Wunschkonzert*, however, the scene is interrupted. The crowd murmur becomes a roar, the music moves to a crescendo, and the couple look off-screen together towards the source of this wave of sound. The camera aligns audience point of view with that of Inge and Herbert together in a shot of the backs of an eager crowd straining for a view into the stadium. We understand now the source of their excitement: the *Führer* has arrived! We follow the couple again as they rush together into the stadium, and watch from their implied perspective as the fiction merges with a montage of propaganda footage: Hitler's motorcade, the *Führer's* entrance, arms raised in greeting, a child's floral gift.

What is significant here is not so much the simple juxtaposition of two apparently incompatible representational modes – propaganda and romantic melodrama – as the way in which the audience's desire for an object of sexual longing (Inge) is deflected, by means of point-of-view editing in particular, towards the *Führer* as a more appropriate focus of erotic interest. This displacement of eroticism from romance to politics is, moreover, sustained throughout the film. Significantly, this is the very last time that we will participate (however briefly) in anything approaching a sexually charged exchange of looks between Herbert and Inge. When the couple later get to meet at all – as they do in any case only infrequently – we are distanced from any sexual intensity by the use of objective camera and the long take. As in the second half of the sequence discussed above, the couple tend to be filmed in two-shot at medium distance: close-up and shot-reverse shot are used only for rare moments of antagonistic confrontation – when Herbert accuses Inge of unfaithfulness, for instance.

That apparent inhibiting of audience pleasure in the love narrative operates in stark contrast with the visual treatment of the audience relationship to the athletes, and of course to the *Führer* as he makes his long-awaited entrance. From the outset, our gaze is aligned with that of the expectant crowd, and we enter with them into the excitement of the occasion. Point-of-view cutting is extensively used in this sequence, not to situate the female protagonist as the object of erotic desire, but to orchestrate our encounter with the objects of an assumed collective or national longing. That same displacement of the eroticised look from the female protagonist, to fascist spectacle, recurs moreover throughout the film – in the erotic presentation of men in uniform, for instance, or in the staging of air battles that are watched with awe and wonder from ground level.

4 The new film history: the canon displaced

Unlike classic accounts of propaganda that focus only on political content, with little understanding of how that content gains popular appeal, close formal analysis of even this very brief passage from *Wunschkonzert* can thus begin to show how the film involves the spectator in an emotional, indeed a quasi-erotic relationship with filmic objects of political desire: the soldier, the Aryan athlete, the *Führer* and so on. But the shift I have been describing to film-critical interest in issues of spectatorship doesn't stop with the textual analysis of strategies of address: it has also raised larger questions about what texts are chosen in the first place as representative of German cinema at any given moment.

In the histories that have established as canonical a limited number of texts from the three exemplary periods identified at the beginning of this article, the selection of any film for inclusion in the pantheon of German cinema has been based, as we saw, largely on either aesthetic or political/ideological judgements. In histories more closely concerned with audience reception, by contrast, the emphasis shifts to films that held special appeal to specific groups of historical spectators. In relation to Weimar, for example, historians studying contemporary accounts of film culture and audience response have noted the particular attraction of the film medium for women in the period; and their work has brought to the foreground of Weimar film history such hitherto neglected, though at the time hugely popular comedies as Lubitsch's *The doll* and the comedy *The oyster princess* (Hake, 1993), or such classical melodramas as Pabst's *Die freudlose Gasse* or Grüne's *Dirnentragödie* (Petro, 1989). The same displacement of critical attention from a handful of works seen as crystalline examples of the spirit of national cinema at any given moment, to popular genre films with mass appeal, is evident in recent work on Nazi cinema: thus the late Karsten Witte, in one seminal overview of the field, expresses relief at the shift in focus of recent criticism away from ' *ein Dutzend ostentativer Propagandafilmè* and towards genre films whose study permits a more differentiated understanding of the relationship between National Socialist politics and popular pleasures (Witte, 1993 p.119).

It is not yet clear what impact the new film history may have on German Studies curricula and classroom practice. Certainly, it offers a range of new approaches to canonical texts. The various recent histories referenced above have in common that they view the film text through the eyes of contemporary audiences: audiences who bring to the film a vast array of public and private desires, fears and anxieties. That there is rich historical insight to be gained from this reception-oriented perspective is amply demonstrated by recent re-readings of the Weimar art film: Anton Kaes' study of Weimar Expressionism as a response to the traumas of the Great War, for instance, or Stephen Schindler's work on Murnau and masculinity (Kaes, 1998; Schindler, 1996).

Further, if the art film is re-historicised in the new film history, then the propaganda film – read traditionally as if formally indistinguishable from political rhetoric – is re-aestheticised, re-established as an art form deserving of critical analysis and close attention to textual detail. Thus I have tried to show in my reading of *Wunschkonzert* how formal analysis of even the crudest propaganda text can make clearer than can any account of manifest content its historical function in engaging and channelling popular desire.

The final implication of a film-historical approach centred on spectatorship and reception is that the range of texts we teach must be expanded. But there are practical hurdles to be overcome. One key issue is the restricted nature of available resources; we are hampered by limitations on films available for hire on 16mm, as well as by the even more restricted range of subtitled video, and/or of supplementary materials to help students poor in language to understand a German film in an unsubtitled version. This article offers no solution to pragmatic issues of this nature – however urgent I may believe them to be. It is intended, by contrast, simply as an invitation: an invitation to a

92

more pluralistic engagement with German film culture that may bring new insights – and at times, unexpected pleasures – to the teaching of German cinema.

Bibliography

Albrecht G, *Die großen Filmerfolge. Vom Blauen Engel bis Amadeus* (Ebersberg, Edition 8½ Just, 1985)

Eisner L, *The haunted screen. Expressionism in the German cinema and the influence of Max Reinhardt* (London, Secker and Warburg, 1973)

Elsaesser T, 'Film history and visual pleasure: Weimar history' in: Mellencamp P, et al (eds.) *Cinema histories, cinema practices* (Los Angeles, University Publications of America, pp.54–81, 1984)

————. 'Lulu and the meter man: Louise Brooks, Pabst and *Pandora's Box*' in: *Screen* (vol. 24, no. 4–5, pp.4–36, 1983)

————. ed. *A second life: German cinema's first decades* (Amsterdam, Amsterdam University Press, 1996)

————. 'Social mobility and the fantastic: German silent cinema' in: Donald J, ed. *Fantasy and the cinema* (London, BFI, pp.10–22, 1989)

Fuhrmann S, 'Die pfeifende "Traumbraut"' in: Rother R, ed. *Wunschkonzert.* Ufa-Magazin (vol.17, Berlin, Deutsches Historisches Museum, 1992)

Hake S, 'The oyster princess and the doll: Wayward women of early silent cinema' in: Frieden S, et al (eds) *Gender and German cinema: Feminist interventions, Part II* (Providence, RI, Berg, pp.13–32, 1993)

————. *Passions and deceptions: the early films of Ernst Lubitsch* (Princeton, Princeton University Press, 1992)

Hansen M, 'Early cinema – whose public sphere?' in: Elsaesser T and A Barker (eds) *Early cinema. Space, frame, narrative* (London, BFI, pp.228–246, 1990)

Horkheimer M and T W Adorno, *Dialektik der Aufklärung. Philosophische Fragmente* (Frankfurt am Main, Fischer, 1971)

Kaes A, *Shell shock: Film and trauma in Weimar Germany* (Princeton, Princeton University Press, 1998)

Kracauer S, *From Caligari to Hitler: a psychological history of the German film* (Princeton, Princeton University Press, 1947)

Mayne J, *Cinema and spectatorship* (London and New York, Routledge, 1993)

Petro P, *Joyless streets. Women and melodramatic representation in Weimar Germany* (Princeton, Princeton University Press, 1989)

Rentschler E, *The ministry of illusion. Nazi cinema and its afterlife* (Cambridge, Mass., Harvard University Press, 1996)

Schindler S, 'What makes a man a man: the construction of masculinity in F W Murnau's *The last laugh*' in: *Screen* (vol. 37, no. 1, pp.30–40, 1996)

Schlüpmann H, *Unheimlichkeit des Blicks. Das Drama des frühen deutschen Kinos* (Frankfurt am Main, Stroemfeld/Roter Stern, 1990)

Silberman M, *German cinema: Texts and contexts* (Detroit, Michigan, Wayne State University Press, 1995)

Welch D, *Propaganda and the German cinema 1933–1945* (Oxford, Oxford University Press, 1983)

Witte K, 'Film im Nationalsozialismus. Blendung und Überblendung' in: Jacobsen W, et al (eds.) *Geschichte des deutschen Films* (Stuttgart, Metzler, pp.119–170, 1993)

6 | Landscape, ideology and national identity in the German cinema: A case study of *Die goldene Stadt* (1942)

Alasdair King
University of Portsmouth

1 Introduction

In his recent essay, *German cultural history and the study of film: ten theses and a postscript,* Anton Kaes (1995, p.49) makes a convincing case for studying the German cinema as part of a complex cultural history. His main argument can be summarised in his claim that 'films signify something not *in abstracto,* but concretely at a certain moment in time, at a certain place, and for a certain audience'. This assertion is part of a general critical approach to the German cinema which takes into account the numerous different histories – economic, political, social, technological as well as aesthetic – which define the moments of a film's production, distribution and reception. Central to Kaes's cultural-historical model are certain questions which participate in ongoing debates in German cinema on ideology and national identity (1995, p.50):

> *How does film construct and negotiate national identity? How can one articulate the relationship between a film and its historical and cultural context? How does film function in the self-fashioning of a national culture?*

Although the set of questions proposed by Kaes can be applied fruitfully to any period in German cinema, they promise a useful way of negotiating the large and varied body of work produced under National

Socialism between 1933 and 1945. In order to understand the workings of this cinema in more depth, and to progress beyond the understandable but unproductive desire to dismiss wholesale the most problematic period in German film history, it is necessary to explore more closely how certain films constructed national identity at this time and, just as importantly, how audiences related (and relate today) to these images and narratives. Central to this is the need to explore the extent to which cinema in the Third Reich set out to fashion a national culture and, crucially, to investigate from the perspective of the 1990s the status of National Socialist films in the development of Germany's national cinema.

The following examination of *Die goldene Stadt* (1942) addresses these questions. Although it has not yet received a great deal of critical attention, the film occupies a pivotal place in the history of National Socialist, and, by extension, German film production. At an immediate level, it serves to remind viewers that the majority of films made under National Socialism shared neither the visual look nor the unsubtle propaganda messages of films such as Riefenstahl's *Triumph des Willens* (1935), which are often taken as representative of the period. This is in no way to deny that *Die goldene Stadt* draws on National Socialist ideology: it is indelibly marked by the political climate of its production and in particular by its engagement with questions of national identity and by its complex portrayal of preferred gender roles. Its ideological messages are communicated both through the dialogue and also through the visual composition of particular sequences. With this in mind, it is important to analyse the use of *mise-en-scène*, particularly the way the film constructs a landscape of the *Heimat* or home/homeland to stress a particular German identity which has clear ideological connotations. In its aesthetics of landscape, *Die goldene Stadt* occupies an important point in the history of the *Heimatfilm* genre in Germany, borrowing as it does from aspects of *Blut und Boden* films and yet working in close relation to, even anticipating, elements of the 1950s *Heimatfilm* which possibly accounts for its successful revivals in this decade.

However, the relationship between *Die goldene Stadt* and a number of different strands of National Socialist thinking is complex and ambiguous, not least because its status as a vehicle for purveying Nazi ideology, especially concerning national identity, is tempered by other considerations. It is essential to note how national identity plays a role not just in the representations within the film. *Die goldene Stadt,* as a successful product of the domestic film industry, is central to the identity of the German cinema itself under National Socialism on account of its status as a blockbuster 'Made in Germany'. It is easy to overlook the encouragement under National Socialism of the development of a massive popular cinema produced in Germany to rival Hollywood with big budgets, production values, stars and large attendances. It is in this context that *Die goldene Stadt* is so significant because it utilised cinematic conventions and technical developments in colour film photography in such a way that, at the time it was released, it proved to be phenomenally popular. It broke box office records nearly everywhere it played in Germany, and was also a major hit in France, Spain, Sweden, Bulgaria, Austria, Switzerland, Norway, Latvia, Holland, Poland, Belgium – even Buenos Aires – attracting people to the cinema who never visited it in the normal course of events. This success played a large part in forcing cinemas to change their normal practices of ticket booking and performance schedules to cope with the demand for tickets.[29]

It is hardly possible, then, to understand the ideological operations of *Die goldene Stadt* as a film without thinking historically about the audiences' engagement with its attractions as a cinematic event or spectacle. In this respect *Die goldene Stadt* reopens questions which are at the heart of some of the most recent research on National Socialist cinema, namely the need to account for the way that many films of this period offer clear ideological support to National Socialist policies without forfeiting the viewing pleasures of cinema audiences during the war, which were composed of a more differentiated spectrum of opinion than simply card-carrying members of the Nazi Party (Rentschler, 1990, pp.260–262). The obvious questions which follow

---

29 *'Vom Vorverkauf zum Stammsitz', Film-Kurier,* 24 February 1943, p.2, and ' *Von dem Siegeszug der* Goldenen Stadt', *Film-Kurier,* 31 March 1943, p.4, give details of cinema attendances and changes in ticketing practices.

from this are also the hardest to answer: how exactly were the ideological aspects of this kind of production made into visually attractive and compelling cinema? What precisely made this kind of film so attractive to cinema audiences at this time? Are the ideological and aesthetic aspects of films like *Die goldene Stadt* inseparable, or can they resonate differently for different audiences at different times?

2 *Die goldene Stadt* as national ideology

Die goldene Stadt was passed by the National Socialist censor on 7 August 1942 with the predicate of ' *künstlerisch besonders wertvoll* (of particular artistic merit) rather than with any of the alternative predicates, which included 'politically valuable'. It was released as suitable only for an adult audience and had its German premiere in Berlin on 24 November 1942. However, it had been introduced to the public initially at the Biennale festival in Venice at the beginning of September that year, where it received immediate acclaim. The Venice festival had become the only international platform which remained for German films and so the launch of *Die goldene Stadt* was considered important enough for Goebbels to attend to promote the film. Its director, Veit Harlan, was awarded the International Film Chamber prize and its star (and Harlan's wife), Kristina Söderbaum, who attended in her peasant costume from the film, received the Coppa Volpa for best actress for her performance. Harlan was one of the best-known filmmakers at work under National Socialism and was awarded the prestigious title of professor by Goebbels in appreciation, according to Harlan's autobiography, of *Die goldene Stadt*.[30]

Although Harlan is nowadays more often remembered for his infamous historical dramas, *Jud Süß* and *Kolberg*, all of his melodramas, according to Karsten Witte, make a key contribution to the cinema of the Third Reich. They follow closely the contours of National Socialist domestic

---

30 According to Harlan, Goebbels awarded him the *professorship* after praising ' *den größten Erfolg, den die Ufa jemals gehabt hatte, meinen Film* Die goldene Stadt' (Harlan, 1966, p.155). See also Harlan's document, 'My Attitude towards National Socialism', in the *Deutsches Institut für Filmkunde* (no further references), an attempt to justify his actions in his defence against Allied charges, where he notes 'Goebbels, on that occasion, emphasized that I was being awarded that distinction in appreciation of my best film, *Die goldene Stadt'* (p.12).

and foreign policies and were highly valued by the regime, not least because of the financial returns from the films outside Germany (Witte, 1980). Given his ability to make films quickly and efficiently which both adhered to current National Socialist policies and which were almost certain to succeed at the box office, it is not difficult to see why Harlan held such a privileged position in Nazi film production. However, there has not been much attention paid to the close analysis of what made the series of films which featured the Harlan/Söderbaum combination, running from *Jugend* (1938) to *Immensee* (1943) and *Opfergang* (1944), so successful in their ability to adhere in differing degrees to National Socialist ideology and also to prove so attractive for viewers in different countries.[31]

In the case of *Die goldene Stadt*, Harlan conforms largely to the structure of conventional melodramas where a young woman negotiates a path from the family home into a wider, adult world, and it exhibits the number of twists typical of that genre, before settling for a tragic, rather than the more conventional happy, ending. It begins on the large farm of the *Großbauer* Jobst on the banks of the Moldau river in the German-speaking area of Czechoslovakia, the Sudetenland. The farmer's daughter, Anna (played by Kristina Söderbaum), has a yearning to visit the 'golden city', Prague, a yearning which is neither assuaged by her indulgent treatment at the hands of her father, nor her lengthy engagement to the loving and down-to-earth farmworker, Thomas. The audience learns that Anna's mother, who had come from the city, was also obsessed with returning to Prague and had drowned in the nearby marshes some years before as she attempted to leave. Anna's existence is further destabilised by the presence of the engineer, Leitwein, who is supposed to drain the marshes for agricultural use and who gives her a present of a picture book of Prague.

Anna's father dismisses her curiosity about the 'golden city', but she sets out for Prague when her father and Thomas are away on business. In Prague she visits her Czech aunt, Donata, who has an illegitimate son, Toni. Although she is attracted to Leitwein, who she meets again in

---

31 An important exception is the recent article on *Opfergang* (1944) by Mary-Elizabeth O'Brien (1995). *Die goldene Stadt* is discussed at some length in Traudisch (1993) and Lowry (1991).

Prague, Toni tells her that the engineer is married. He takes advantage of her distress to seduce her, preventing her from getting back to her village before her absence is noted by her returning father.

Anna, remaining in Prague, discovers that she is pregnant and is disinherited by her father. Toni, who had wanted to inherit the land through marrying Anna, also disowns her. She returns home to be rejected by her father. She meets with the same fate as her mother as she drowns herself in the marshes. Filled with remorse, the father then has the marshes drained and Thomas, Anna's former fiance, inherits the now fertile land.

Although there are elements in *Die goldene Stadt* which are recycled from earlier Harlan/Söderbaum films such as *Jugend* with the punishment of Söderbaum's character for carrying an illegitimate child, and *Verwehte Spuren* where she is lost in a threatening city, the basic source for the new film was the successful stageplay, *Der Gigant* (1937) by Richard Billinger which Harlan and Alfred Braun adapted. It was given a clear ideological twist in the adaptation in that although all the characters in the play are German, Harlan's film attempts to draw a contrast between the good Sudeten German farmers and the less attractive characters in Prague, Toni, Donata and Toni's employer and mistress, Frau Tandler, who are now depicted as Czech, as is the manipulative Maruschka who lives on the *Hof*. This change ensured that one aspect of the question of national identity in the *Großdeutsches Reich*, namely the tensions between the German-speaking population and the Czechs in the Sudetenland, Bohemia and Prague itself were immediately brought to the fore.

Prior to Germany's annexation of Czechoslovakia in 1938 there had been three-and-a-quarter million German-speaking inhabitants and some seven and a quarter million Czechs in the Republic, in addition to a number of other ethnic groups. Most of the Germans were located in the industrial region, the Sudetenland, where phases of high unemployment borne mostly by the Germans, and increasingly nationalist sentiments on both German and Czech sides had led to the deep unrest exploited by Hitler as the pretext for invasion.

Official German attitudes towards the Czech population varied depending on current policy, but the popular German representation of the Czech as 'a half-educated [...] creature, [...] politically intolerable and unreliable, socially never satisfied' (Thorne, 1967, pp.54–56 and Henig, 1985, pp.32–33) finds its parallels in the representation, albeit comic at times, of Toni, devious, manipulative, promiscuous and upwardly mobile. In fact, in many ways the portrayal of the Czech characters is similar to the portrayal of Jews in other National Socialist films: untrustworthy, decadent and immoral (Barten, 1993). In this way, the film participates in one of the central ideological thrusts of National Socialism, that of differentiating between the racially pure German native and the racially other, the inferior, in National Socialist eyes, whether Jew or Slav.

One of the major strands of this ideology was the rigour with which the purity of the German national stock in all its forms, biological and geographical, had to be defended, and why the theme of inheritance is so persistent in the film. Not only is the German woman, Anna, seduced and therefore in National Socialist terms 'contaminated' by the Czech Toni, who has inherited his parents' racially-determined traits of decadence and immorality, but as a result she finds she is carrying a mixed-race child who stands to inherit German soil. Harlan records how, despite the considerable added expense, Goebbels intervened in the post-production phase to insist that the film's planned ending be reshot to culminate in the death of Anna, not so much to punish her misdemeanours, although that played a role, but to kill off her unborn child in order to ensure that, in Goebbels' words, the ' *Tschechenbalg* ' would not inherit the land after the reconciliation of Anna and her father, the ending preferred by Harlan (Harlan, 1966). In fact, the *Hof* ultimately passed to the pure, rooted German, Thomas, who had been accepted as a son by the *Bauer*. This racial-political reading is reinforced by looking at one of the few documents to record immediate reactions to the film, where the head of police and leading member of the SS in Belgrade wrote after the Serbian premiere recommending that the film not be shown in areas where Slavs could see it: ' *Der Film zeigt direkt den Slaven, wie man es machen muß und wie leicht trotz der Rassenpropaganda der Einbruch in eine deutsche Bauernfamilie gelingt* ' (reproduced in Wulf, 1966, pp.350–51).

Prague occupies a complex position in this national geography. In the film, it is neither demonised as the great modern international metropolis, prey to mass working-class movements and Jewish ghettoes, as large cities are in many National Socialist films, nor is it really a place dominated by the negative 'Czech' traits mentioned earlier. True, the city is the scene of Anna's downfall, rather than the German countryside, but Prague itself is shown as a city of culture and history – we are taken to the opera, for example – as well as a space in which lurk elements of the alien, the non-German. If representations of the city in Nazi cinema often depict either the horrors of the modern, non-German city, or show how a German city is exposed to the danger of foreign penetration (Schulte-Sasse, 1990)[32], then the depiction of Prague in *Die goldene Stadt* in fact has more in common with the latter model than the former. This can be explained ideologically perhaps because in the eyes of many Germans, Prague was not seen as a foreign cultural space, but instead it was perceived to be at heart a German city. In his diaries, Goebbels recounts a visit in 1940 (Taylor, 1992, pp.165–66):

> *Drive through glorious Prague, which is a wholly German city. All buildings, bridges and towers are evidence of it [...] Tour the city. What a jewel. St Vitus' Cathedral with all its treasures. The old buildings, streets and squares. The view over the Moldau. An unforgettable sight. I have fallen totally in love with this city. It exudes the German spirit and must become German again one day.*

Goebbels' list of sights finds its visual form in the film when the audience sees Anna's tour of the 'golden' city, a tour which makes extensive use of location shooting at all the sites noted above. One way of thinking about *Die goldene Stadt* is then to place it in the context of Goebbels' desire to reinforce claims to the German status of Prague rather than to dwell on its foreignness, and in accord with this, to highlight the dangers of the contamination, on a geographical as well as a biological level, of the German national body by Czech or Slav influences. This helps to explain one of the discrepancies of the film: although city life in general is disparaged in the dialogue, in terms of

---

32 As is clear from my subsequent argument, I disagree with Schulte-Sasse's implication that Prague represents in *Die goldene Stadt* an unequivocally foreign space.

visual representation, Prague offers up its sights to the German audience as a trophy worth defending against the racially inferior Czech population. The corruption of the city is shown only in interior scenes, in bars and in the *Tabakladen* owned by the aunt. The external shots of the city act to confirm, rather than contradict, the 'goldene Stadt' of Anna's reveries, even though male characters as different as her father, Leitwein and Toni all tell her that the reality of Prague is very different from how she imagines it.

Despite the desire of the Nazi authorities to maximise revenue by exhibiting the film as widely as possible, and although the film was released to great acclaim in many parts of Europe, there is contradictory evidence about whether it was exhibited in Czechoslovakia. There are some accounts which suggest that it had an early showing in Prague, but others indicate that it was banned in the Sudetengau. Amongst the wealth of press reports of the film's success in many parts of occupied and neutral Europe, there are none recording its reception in Czechoslovakia at all which suggests that it was considered simply too provocative on the question of national identity in what was still a turbulent region.[33]

Next to the ideological promotion of German identity and *Lebensraum* against Czech claims, the most important single political theme in *Die goldene Stadt* concerns the question of *Landflucht* or the inclination of those in the country to leave the land for the questionable attractions of the city. Even before the outbreak of the war, this had been a serious problem for the authorities, as, despite the high ideological value placed on *Heimat* and the soil, rural deprivation and the amenities and opportunities in large cities had ensured a massive depopulation of the land. With most of the male Germans needed for the war effort away from the countryside, the burden of agricultural work fell to an even greater extent on women (Grünberger, 1971). Party propagandists regularly targeted women in rural areas, who were felt to be largely responsible for the exodus, reprimanding them for their susceptibility

---

33 In Michele Sakkara's (1980, pp.146–47) notes on the film, it is listed as premiering in Prague on 24 November 1942, which was actually the occasion of its German premiere in Berlin. There were no records in *Film-Kurier* or other German newspapers from the period 1942–45 to substantiate Sakkara's claim.

to, as Grünberger (1971, p.161) puts it, 'the glitter of city life'. *Die goldene Stadt* must be understood in this context. Harlan records telling Goebbels before the film was made that it, would not be apolitical, as Goebbels had previously maintained, but that it would have a political theme as it dealt with the problem of *Landflucht*. This theme is clear in, for example, the statements of the farmer Jobst, who says:

> *Die Stadt, die lassen wir den Leuten, die da leben müssen. Wir sind da auf dem Land. Geh'n ja so viele Menschen vom Land in die Stadt, denken, da liegt das Geld auf der Straße. Sie können aber auf dem Pflaster gar nicht leben, weil sie da nicht geboren sind.*

The widespread desire to leave the harsh rural environment and to experience the fantasy of the city is a key element in understanding how the film works. It is Anna's story, of course, at the most immediate level, but it is in some ways also the ideological journey of the viewers. The film opens in very knowing fashion by offering the spectacle of the glittering 'golden city' directly to the audience in the form of Leitwein's picture book, which parades the visual temptations of the imaginary city before the eager eyes of the wartime film public. Eric Rentschler (1993, pp.39–40) has argued that one recurrent practice in the feature films made under National Socialism is the granting of a wish 'in order to vanquish wishful thinking'. [34] This seems applicable both to Anna, whose wish to visit Prague ends in disaster, and her willing return to her village, but also to the members of the audience, many of whom might also harbour desires to experience the thrills of the big city.

Anna's desire to see Prague, a character flaw inherited from her wayward mother, is forcefully articulated in her statement of independence:

> *Ich will leben, wie ich will, ich will heiraten, wenn ich will. Ich will was haben von meinem Leben.*

Her last words, after the granting of her wish, show her realisation of

---

34 Rentschler uses this phrase in his discussion of Luis Trenker's *Der Verlorene Sohn* (1934) – it is interesting to think of Anna in the context of Trenker's film as the prodigal daughter of Nazi cinema.

her folly and remorse for imagining that the grass could be greener away from home:

Du hast recht gehabt, Vater, bis zum letzten. [...] Vater, vergib mir, daß ich die Heimat nicht so liebte wie du.

According to Harlan (1966), Anna's final speech was another change instigated by the intervention of Goebbels. The audience's desire for the glitter of the city, which is acknowledged in the opening sequence with the series of shots from the picture book, can hardly be punished as Anna is for her ideologically-transgressive yearning. Instead there is an attempt at the visual level to satisfy the desire for golden imagery through the closing shots which show the marsh after it has been drained to allow rows of golden, waving corn to grow. In this way there is an attempt to accommodate the audience's desire by displacing it back to the *Heimat*, the countryside, but this time not to the harsh and threatening marshes, but to a fertile golden landscape. The wishful thinking of many members of the audience to relinquish the burdens of rural life is not directly vanquished but thus rechannelled into a revaluation of the potential rewards of remaining in the countryside. Whether this strategy worked or not is impossible to tell, of course. However, in this context it is worth noting that, while the film was a major hit everywhere it played, as the *Film-Kurier* of 31 March 1943 reports (p.4), it was a phenomenal success in rural cinemas, where the yearnings to experience the 'glitter' of the city might presumably be strongest.

In addition to the desire for the spectacle which unites Anna with the wartime audience, many Germans would also have been able to understand her obsessive quest for her roots, her real *Heimat*. For those Germans who had been displaced by the war – forced to move either through bombings in their home cities or through having to serve far from home – Anna's restlessness in the village and yearning to experience the topography mapped by her mother's life in Prague would more likely have been perceived sympathetically than condemned (a similar reading is attributed to Martin Loiperdinger in Barten, 1993). It was National Socialist policy to show new films as widely as possible, not just in the biggest cities but simultaneously in remote areas and for soldiers in the *Frontkinos* near to the areas of fighting. The immediate success of *Die goldene Stadt* might well have been in part owing to its release just before Christmas where its ability to offer a compensatory sense of *Heimat* for those displaced would have been most effective.

The importance of the topography of *Heimat,* countryside and city in defining and differentiating national identities, largely through emphasis on the positive features of the German community versus alien values, has been discussed, but the film also takes care to utilise these spaces to reinforce desirable gender roles and appropriate sexual identities. Despite wartime conditions, which ensured the relatively greater independence and mobility of many women workers (and the danger that they might be in close contact with foreign labourers while the German men were away at the war), the film's plot ensures the ultimate punishment of Anna for not conforming to accepted notions of feminine behaviour. Her yearning to see the city is part of a more general desire to attain independence from the patriarchal authority of the male figures surrounding her. Anna's independence is initially portrayed positively, though it is an attribute which could so easily become recklessness as is shown in the scenes depicting her ability to drive the coach at great speed without Leitwein's assistance and to perform better than most of the men in the horse race at the local fair. It is hinted early in the film that this independent streak might be Anna's downfall, especially because it includes elements of an independent sexuality which threaten the order of the *Heimat* established by her father. She is not only attracted to Prague in defiance of her father's wishes, but initially also to Leitwein, rather than to Thomas, her father's choice. This is emphasised in her insistence on wearing a dress to the fair that will allow her to dance freely rather than be, in her words, like a wedding dress, which would mark her out as a bride. Her slip as she runs to meet Leitwein and the snake that slithers across the marshes are early warning signals that in her sexual desires lie great danger. The film makes repeated reference to inappropriate female behaviour, from the desertion of the family by Anna's own mother to the depiction of Aunt Donata in Prague. The use of colour film stock plays an important role in coding the *mise-en-scène* as Donata's garish dresses are in sharp contrast to Anna's innocent peasant frock. Anna's change of costume in Prague where she is transformed from the confident but naive country girl into a modish city dweller has her instead looking awkwardly overdressed – she is not comfortable with the veil of her dress – and over made-up, reinforcing visually her fall from the ordered and moral *Heimat*, and leaving her closer in appearance to Donata and Frau Tandler than she would like, a visual reminder that this might be her fate if she remains in the city.

Whereas the representations of femininity revolve around issues of sexuality, masculinities are differentiated in terms of the relationship of the male characters to tradition and modernity. The *Hof* is dominated by the farmer Jobst, who enjoys total authority over both his family, the other labourers and the engineers from outside the *Heimat*. His power is akin to a kind of natural law which finds its articulation in his statements about the cruel but just retributive effect of the marshes. Jobst's *Blut-und-Boden* authoritarianism tries to maintain the order of the *Heimat*, but is ultimately revealed to be inflexible and destructive, as it ends in the death of his daughter. His agrarian traditionalism clashes not only with the wishes and desires of Anna but also with the modernising drive of the engineers. This clash parallels the major discrepancy in National Socialist thinking between the anti-modern ideologies of men like Rosenberg and the technocratic impulses of officials like Speer.

Although he is from the big city, Prague, Leitwein is represented in a generally positive light throughout the film as someone who can successfully negotiate both the spaces of the city and, through his profession, the landscape of the *Heimat*. He recognises Anna's desires and encourages her to think for herself beyond the authoritarian discourse of her father. In his comments that ' *Wer nie fortkommt, kommt nie heim*' and his offer of a protected tour through Prague, he opens up a route whereby she could, in his view, safely act on her desires. Anna's rejection of this route indicates that, in her mind, it compromises her independence as much as the direct authoritarianism of her father.

Finally, the figure of Thomas should not be overlooked in the analysis of male gender roles. Like Leitwein, he combines a feel for the land with the flexibility to impose reform where it might be needed. Whereas Leitwein's successful urban modernity is shown in the attention paid to his car in Prague, Thomas's forward-thinking is symbolised in the film through his use of the latest agricultural technology. His successes are ultimately greater, as his reward for reconciling the opposing poles of the *Heimat* and modernity is to inherit the *Hof* which is drained and proves fertile and profitable. Rudolf Prack, cast here as Thomas, occupies an important place in the representation of German masculinity not just under National Socialism but also, and significantly, after the war. He reappears, opposite Sonja Ziemann, in a number of *Heimatfilme* of the early 1950s playing the reliable German male who had successfully negotiated a new male identity out of the devastation of the war.

3 Die *goldene Stadt* and its audiences

Die goldene Stadt actually became the most successful feature film made under National Socialism. Audiences totalled 42 million between the end of 1942 and the end of 1944 and it brought in 12 million *Reichsmark* from German cinemas alone, where some 30 million visits to the film were made. The total revenue brought in by the film rises to nearly 30 million *Reichsmark* when foreign sales are included, having cost a comparatively modest (when one takes into account the expense of shooting in colour) 2 million *Reichsmark* to produce. Statistics from film industry accounts list exact numbers of visitors and suggest that even after the initial surge to see the film when it opened, it managed to retain its popularity with audiences well into 1945. [35]

One of the most difficult challenges to film historians is to find sufficient evidence to account for trends and shifts in popular taste. The increasing popularity of the cinema as a way of escaping the stark realities of what was proving to be anything but the short, decisive, victorious war promised (Beyer, 1992), can give some general information that many films were well-attended in the early 1940s, but this says little about the particular attractions of *Die goldene Stadt*. Less

---

[35] I am grateful to Dr.Gerd Albrecht at the Deutsches Instiut für Filmkunde, Frankfurt, for allowing me to see this information in the *Ufa-Geschäftsbücher*.

is known about the viewing pleasures of the audiences during National Socialism than either during the Weimar period or after the war because such information was rarely deemed worth collecting by either the Nazi administration or by the film industry. The only reports made on the reactions of audiences were by the *Sicherheitsdienst* in attempts to gauge the effectiveness of a small number of specific politically important films. As *Die goldene Stadt* did not come into this category, it is more difficult to trace its reception with this kind of precision.

It was marketed as a Veit Harlan film, on the strength of the reputation of the director, and as a vehicle for Kristina Söderbaum, who belonged to a small but diverse band of female stars in the Third Reich. In his autobiography, Veit Harlan suggests that *Die goldene Stadt* struck such a popular chord because of four elements, namely the strength of Billinger's original play; the use in the film of Smetana's *Bartered bride*, the acting, particularly of Kristina Söderbaum; and finally the use of colour in the film.

The precise significance of Söderbaum to German audiences at this time is interesting – she was often cast as an impulsive, naive child-woman whose behaviour normally led to her having to be sacrificed at the end of the film to pay for her sins, an act which German audiences, familiar with the National Socialist discourse of self-sacrifice for the good of the Reich, could recognise. As a Söderbaum trademark was a semi-naked appearance in or near water, this sacrifice was often carried out through death by drowning, a habit which earned her the nickname the '*Reichswasserleiche*' [state water corpse].

However, it is the use of colour which is most often remarked upon in newspaper reviews of the film in the early 1940s. The development of the colour film should be seen as fulfilling two important roles in the national cinema of Nazi Germany. The feature film was promoted heavily by Goebbels in 1942 and after as a way of offering both distraction from the war and from the administration's failure to fulfil its promises to provide a variety of modern cultural products and to stimulate mass consumption in Germany. A technically proficient mass culture, of which the colour film was an intrinsic part, would act to offer compensation for these failures (Schütz, 1995). Moreover, it would increase the international competitiveness, particularly with regard to Hollywood, of the German film industry as an exporter to neutral countries (Beyer, 1992). *Die goldene Stadt* provided the breakthrough in this respect as it was the first really successful German colour film, utilising the new technology of Agfacolour to telling effect. The first full-length colour feature, *Frauen sind doch bessere Diplomaten* (1941), had been deemed, by Goebbels particularly, as a failure technically when compared to the quality of Hollywood colour processes, although the film had been fairly successful at the German box office. *Die goldene Stadt*, reaping the benefits of Harlan's extensive collaboration with leading scientific researchers and manufacturers and also his ability to persuade Goebbels to risk further investment in feature-length colour films, was exhibited at the major film industry conference on 'Film und Farbe' in Dresden in October, 1942, where its significance as a milestone in the technical development of the German cinema was immediately recognised and roundly applauded (Grassmann and Rahts, 1943).

The use of colour in *Die goldene Stadt* goes beyond the basic illustration of the story. Colour becomes one of the semiotic elements at play in the clothing of the characters and in the depiction of key events. It also played a role in the editing of the film in that there are unusually long takes for a film of this period (Salt, 1985). This could well be because Harlan didn't want to waste the expensive colour stock and so took great care over the composition of each shot, but the effect of this is to produce beautiful cinematography for the audience and a series of spectacles for the viewing public which hardly advance the plot. This use of colour also contributes to the ideological slippages in the film. It is hard for a director to simultaneously sell to the audience and to the film industry the technology of colour film through a series of magnificent spectacles while also producing visual scenes which show the big city in an unfavourable light. It is very difficult to demonise Prague and at the same time show how proficiently it can be filmed in Agfacolour.

4 *Die goldene Stadt* in the Federal Republic

Despite the initial policies of the Allies, National Socialist cinema did not disappear after the defeat of Germany. Given the status of *Die goldene Stadt* in the marketing of a massive domestic popular cinema and its huge success with German and non-German audiences, it is interesting to outline briefly the paths taken by the film in the postwar period in the Federal Republic. How did audiences in the decades from the 1950s to the 1990s respond to the images and ideology of the film?

As might be expected, most discourse surrounding its revival at different points has concentrated on playing down the ideological aspects highlighted earlier, particularly those concerning contrasts between German national identity and the Czechs. Instead, *Die goldene Stadt* has largely been reclaimed and recuperated either, in popular terms, as a Kristina Söderbaum *Schicksalsdrama,* or, for distributors, as a classic of German cinema history to rank alongside *M* and *Der blaue Engel.* It is often classified as an Ufa film, i.e. made by the Ufa production company, the German '*Traumfabrik*', which allows it to claim a place (albeit a disputed and problematic one) in an aesthetic, rather than political, history of popular German cinema running from 1917 to the postwar period.

Harlan's films were banned by the Allies in the years following Germany's defeat, but a questionnaire carried out by the American military authorities in Bavaria in 1945 indicated that it was the film made under National Socialism that the public most wanted to see reissued (Lowry, 1991). Plans to revive it in Austria in 1949 had been met with anger from the Czech authorities on the grounds that it was extremely insulting to Czechoslovakia. Nevertheless, when its German release was discussed in 1953, a reference written by Prof. Dr. Walter Hagemann of Münster in its favour (now held in the Frankfurt archives), argued that the Germans were in no way represented more favourably than the Czechs. He claimed that he knew of no other film where the peaceful coexistence of Germans and Czechs was represented so completely without prejudice, especially in comparison with recent Czech *Hetzfilme.* In his view, this was not a nationalistic film and could not offend Czech sensibilities.

The film was released in 1954 – the video copy repeats its opening titles which carry an explanation that it had been in storage – to renewed success. Some press reports indicate protests against Harlan and Söderbaum, who often toured to promote the film. Harlan and Söderbaum's reputation was on the wane, despite the renewed popularity of *Die goldene Stadt.* What is interesting is the way that a number of newspapers actually recommended it to Sudeten Germans who had been resettled in the Federal Republic after the war as a way of seeing their true *Heimat* once more. Yet again, it would seem, filmic spectacle was employed as compensation for what had been lost. The landscape of the film was clearly being used in a new ideological battle, that of the hardening animosity between East and West in Europe, as Prague now lay behind the Iron Curtain, beyond the reach of West German claims on its treasures. Press notices for the film drew attention to this, noting in the case of the *Siegener Zeitung* of 13 April 1955, better *'die goldene Stadt'* than *'die rote Stadt'*! The film was also described as a forerunner of contemporary (i.e. 1950s) *Heimatfilme,* many of which negotiated such complex and interesting changes in popular German self-understanding at that time.

The film was also revived in the early 1960s as a ' *Kinoevergreen',* when Söderbaum and Harlan again appeared at local premieres. Amongst the papers in the files held by the *Deutsches Institut für Filmkunde* in Frankfurt are several telegrams to the couple from enthusiastic cinema owners which note how the film had preserved its validity, and, revealingly, how performances of *Die goldene Stadt* had sold out, having attracted the old *Stammpublikum* who had not been to the cinema for many years. The owner recorded the public demand for other 'such' films.

In the 1990s, now that the film has been distributed in video format and marketed as an Ufa classic, there is still considerable debate about the general problem of the reshowing of National Socialist films in Germany on television and also in formerly occupied countries (Barten, 1991). With the widespread availability of *Die goldene Stadt* on video, it is useful to return to the questions posed by Anton Kaes considered earlier. How does this film construct and negotiate German identity for its audiences situated in the now-unified Federal Republic? What is the relationship between *Die goldene Stadt* and its changed historical and cultural context? And finally, but crucially, how does it function today in the self-fashioning of a national culture? This is a question which must be addressed on every occasion that films made under National Socialism are revived and exhibited. The general availability of *Die goldene Stadt* as a video alongside classics of the German cinema suggests that the distributors feel confident that contemporary audiences can dismiss the national ideology which permeates the film while appreciating its contribution to a national cinema 'Made in Germany'.

Bibliography

In researching the reception of *Die goldene Stadt*, I drew heavily on reviews and promotional material in *Film-Kurier*, 1942–45, and appropriate editions of *Der Film, Das Reich, Filmwelt, Filmwoche, Farbfilm* and *Der deutsche Film* from 1942 and 1943, as well as a sample of post-war film reviews, all held at the *Deutsches Institut für Filmkunde*, Frankfurt am Main.

Barten E W J, 'GBG Spring Conference, 1990: propaganda and entertainment in the cinema during the Second World War' (10–11 May 1990) in: *Historical Journal of Film, Radio and Television*(vol. 11, no. 1, pp.78–81, 1991)

————. 'Re-encounter with the state water corpse: *Die goldene Stadt* in the Netherlands during the Occupation and the current discussion about the reshowing of Nazi films' in: Schmitt-Sasse J, *Widergänger: Faschismus und Antifaschismus im Film* (Münster, MAkS, 1991)

Beyer F, *Die UFA-Stars im Dritten Reich: Frauen für Deutschland* (Munich, Heyne Verlag, 1992)

Grassmann J and W Rahts, *Film und Farbe: Vorträge gehalten auf der gemeinsamen Jahrestagung 'Film und Farbe' der deutschen Kinotechnischen Gesellschaft e.V.* (Berlin, Max Hesses Verlag, 1943)

Grünberger R, *A social history of the Third Reich* (London, Weidenfeld and Nicolson, 1971)

Harlan V, *Im Schatten meiner Filme* (Sigbert Mohn Verlag, 1966)

Henig R, *The origins of the Second World War* (London, Methuen, 1985)

Kaes A, 'German cultural history and the study of film: Ten theses and a postscript' in: *New German Critique* (vol. 65, Spring/Summer, pp.47–58, 1995)

Lowry S, *Pathos und Politik: Ideologie in Spielfilmen des Nationalsozialismus* (Tübingen, Niemeyer Verlag, 1991)

Möbius H, 'Heimat im nationalsozialistischen Stadtfilm' in: *Augen-Blick* (Marburg, vol. 5, pp.31–44, 1988)

O'Brien M, 'Male conquest of the female continent' in: Veit Harlan's *Opfergang. Monatshefte* (vol. 87, no. 4, pp.431–445, 1995)

Petley J, *Capital and culture: German cinema 1933–45* (London, BFI 1979)

Rentschler E, 'German feature films 1933–1945' in: *Monatshefte* (vol. 82, no. 3, pp.257–266, 1990)

———. 'There's no place like home: Luis Trenker's *The prodigal son*' (1934) in: *New German Critique* (vol. 60, pp.33–56, 1993)

Sakkara M, *Die große Zeit des deutschen Films 1933–45* (Leoni am Starnberger See, Druffel Verlag, 1980)

Salt B, 'Continental manners' in: Hayward S, (ed) *European cinema conference proceedings* (Aston, Aston University Papers, 1985)

Schlüpmann H, 'Faschistische Trugbilder weiblicher Autonomie' in: *Frauen und Film* (vol. 44/45, October, pp.44–66, 1988)

Schulte-Sasse L, 'Retrieving the city as Heimat: Berlin in Nazi Cinema' in: Haxthausen C W, and H Suhr, (eds) *Berlin: Culture and metropolis,* (Minneapolis, University of Minnesota Press, pp.166–186, 1990)

Schütz E, 'Das "Dritte Reich" als Mediendiktatur: Medienpolitik und Modernisierung in Deutschland 1933–1945' in: *Monatshefte* (vol. 87, no. 2, pp.129–150, 1995)

Taylor F (ed) *The Goebbels diaries: 1939–41* (London, Hamish Hamilton, 1982)

Thorne C, *The approach of war: 1938–39* (London, Macmillan, 1967)

Traudisch D, *Mutterschaft mit Zuckerguß?: Frauenfeindliche Propaganda im NS-Spielfilm* (Pfaffenweiler, Centaurus Verlag, 1993)

Witte K, 'Der barocke Faschist: Veit Harlan und seine Filme' in: Corino K, (ed) *Intellektuelle im Bann des Nationalsozialismus* (Hamburg, Hoffmann/Campe, pp.150–164, 1980)

Wulf J, *Theater und Film im Dritten Reich – Eine Dokumentation* (Hamburg, Rowohlt, 1966)

7 | Narcissism and alienation: Mirror-images in the New German Cinema

Andrew Webber
Churchill College, Cambridge

1 Introduction

This paper focuses on mirroring strategies in a number of German films in order to inspect the operative metaphor of the volume title: *Deutschland im Spiegel seiner Filme*. If film is to be conceived as a national mirror, then what sort is it, how exactly does it work, for whom, and in response to what kinds of motives? A first answer to this question is given by Thomas Elsaesser in his authoritative history of New German Cinema. Elsaesser (1989, p.278) observes that for many key filmmakers the history of Germany in the twentieth century is representable only by means of strategic deformations: 'Some of the most interesting films tried to get this history into focus by way of what one might call distorting mirrors: the mirrors of terrorism, of family violence, and of the clinical disintegration of a personality'. Elsaesser suggests, therefore, that we should be wary of treating the *Neuer Deutscher Film* as a straightforward mirror, using a candid camera to produce a mimetic record of the nation and its history. The distorting mirror will be a much more useful metaphor, operating with a different sort of candour, as a means of representation which reflects and reflects upon the distortions inherent in the form of its object. The workings of these distortions will be of particular significance for the concepts of *Heimat, Identität,* and *Ideologie*.

I intend briefly to scrutinise the use of mirror-images in four examples

118

of the New German Cinema: Fassbinder's *Fontane Effi Briest* (1974), Wenders's *Im Lauf der Zeit* (1976), von Trotta's *Die bleierne Zeit* (1981), and Reitz's *Heimat* (1984). These are films made over a period of ten years, with very different shapes and styles, but at the core of each of them is the sort of ambivalent mirror that I have gestured towards in my title, one which co-produces narcissism and alienation both for the protagonists and for the viewer.

A discussion of narcissism is bound to incorporate psychoanalytic considerations. If psychoanalysis has formed such a key theoretical basis for the development of Film Studies, it is largely because of how it can help to expose the more illicit pleasures of cinematic viewing: voyeuristic, fetishistic, and – not least – narcissistic. Film theorists have used the theories of Freud and Lacan to analyse the processes of identification which operate both amongst characters on screen, and between them and the viewer. One of the key functions of the silver or multicolour screen – though by no means a simple one – would seem to be as a mirror for self-projection into fantasy scenarios. A key point of recourse is thus Lacan's account of the Mirror Stage, the phase in which an infant first identifies with its body-image. For Lacan (1977) this primary act of self-identification as image is always haunted by contradiction, and it thus establishes a highly ambivalent model for more complex identifications in later development. As the ' *stade*' of the original French can be read as either phase or stadium – a place of spectacle – so the Mirror Stage can be understood as a site for drama. It initiates a process of self-performance on a sort of mirror-stage.

The cinema screen can be seen as a technical reconstruction of this mirror-stage. The inevitable mismatches between the scenes on show and the viewing fantasy, the criss-crossing of the viewer's identification between different characters on screen, can only mean that the pleasures this mirror gives will be at the price of estrangement. What psychoanalytic theories of narcissism show, above all, is that filmic fantasies of self-projection are always subject to alteration and fragmentation. Which is to say that the narcissistic pleasuring of the viewer is always bound up with forms of alienation as s/he negotiates a subject position vis-à-vis the film-text and its complex relations.

119

This abstract model of cinematic narcissism as it works on the individual spectator is further complicated by issues of cultural political context, involving the specific questions of *Heimat*, identity, and ideology. There is an analysis which would identify the German cinema as a key machine in the production of a culture of narcissism. The work of the Mitscherlichs (1977) and others has served to suggest that the German national psyche in the twentieth century has been driven by forms of more or less pathological narcissism. The captivation of the national psyche in its sanitised mirror-imagery glosses over the suppression and repression of otherness which sustains it. This is a cultural complex which produced at its most terrible – and here I borrow the title of Syberberg's epic film – Hitler as ' *ein Film aus Deutschland*': a nightmarish projection of the specularised image of national identity. Or, less catastrophically, the post-war culture of hygienic self-images, projected in particular through the genre of the *Heimatfilm*.

As Syberberg exposes the narcissistic monstrosity of the mass-produced Hitler 'film' through his strategic distortions, so the films which I would like to review here represent a critique of the culture of narcissism and its cinematic spectacles. This, though, never operates from a position of straightforward detachment. The 'new' filmmakers of the 1970s and 1980s search for new images and stories, but they are always inevitably bound into, and in their turn bind the viewer into, the narcissistic complexes of the culture which they inherit.

If the new German filmmakers have a strategy for achieving a certain degree of freedom from the narcissistic capture of German culture and from the alienation inherent in it, then it is especially through the methodology of alienation of a different kind: variations on the *Verfremdungseffekte* of the Brechtian theatre. Techniques of *Verfremdung* are used to mark the limits of, and breaks within, any ideological spectacle, above all preventing the sort of ready identification of the spectator with the spectacle which is the basic lure of narcissism.

What emerges from these films is a complex combination of these different forms of alienation. The relationship to German culture and to the medium of film is characteristically highly ambivalent. If the *Neuer*

120

Deutscher Film emancipates itself from the more systematic propagation of the culture of narcissism, it often cultivates other forms of narcissism, both thematically and formally. Revolt can easily tip into solipsistic retraction and an excessive admiration of an alienated self, put on show as an image for director and viewer alike to share in. This – we might call it a counter-culture of narcissism – is manifest above all in the cult of the director as auteur, imprinted in the images and the text of his or her films. But there is also a potential for a more self-critical development which might be called counter-narcissism, a procedure which seeks to subvert the domination of the culture of narcissism by means of strategies of alienation, but in so doing negotiates a certain ground for new forms of identification.

The brief readings of the four films in question here will show that the work of counter-narcissism, troubled though it may be by shades of what it works against, represents a significant contribution to the reworking of the German identity.

2 Rainer Werner Fassbinder: *Fontane Effi Briest*

Fassbinder's version of Fontane's novel can be understood as an alienation of the culture of narcissism. On a national cultural level, this film is of course part of the fashion for *Literaturverfilmung* which might suggest the costume-drama adaptation of a nineteenth-century novel to the styles of a new Germany: film as a vehicle for mirroring great works of yesteryear, enabling the viewer to enjoy the nostalgic pleasure of cultural recognition. In fact, it serves to distort the attractions of such a mirror-image, and to work against the grain of the culture industry.

Fontane Effi Briest represents a triangular meeting of characters: the title suggests a sort of merging of author and protagonist, but the third agent is the film-author, reconstructing Fontane's text in his own distinctly auteurist fashion. His intention is less to re-enact a story than to identify with the ambivalent *Haltung* of the original author, adopting a split posture of critical detachment and identification with the fictional world and what it represents (Fassbinder, 1986, p.54). The film-author, in other words, reflects his own aesthetic image into the structures of the literary text and onto that of the author. This self-projection is marked partly by Fassbinder's own voice-over, ventriloquizing, as it were, Fontane's personalised narrative voice. And it is marked in a general sense by the distinctive signature of Fassbinder's cinematic stylisations, and more particularly by the pervasive angling of the film's images through relays of mirrors. The extraordinary inflation of mirroring devices in this film, or perhaps we should call it a – barely motion – picture, has a complex mixture of effects. It adapts and replicates an apparently minor motif from Fontane's novel: the mirror as the frame at once for Effi's narcissistic pleasure and for her self-estrangement (the ' *was anderes*' which embodies the otherness to which she is subject (Fontane, 1984, p.71). The mirrors of Fontane's film reflect this division. They represent a heroine constructed to be narcissistic for the pleasure of a narcissistic culture: the female body styled as an image to reflect the desires of the male gaze. The mirrors which so often mediate the images of this film at once open up a space for the imaginary within the domestic interiors of the late nineteenth-century Prussian household, and reinforce the sense of surveillance, of bodily and mental captivity, which govern it. Mirrors double the effects of framing which are so insistent in the film, to show how totally pictured this society is.

At the same time, the mirror is, of course, a stock device in the organisation of cinematic space, a trick for opening up other dimensions of viewing, classically in dialogue scenes, to divert from standard shot-reverse-shot conventions. In Fassbinder's film, the mirror comes to reflect not only social but also cinematic conventions of style and form into the pictorial space, not least by accentuating the immobilisation of the action. It is the marker of an excessive formalism which foregrounds the artificiality, the constructedness, of both the social environment and the film medium. It interrupts and distances: ' *Erstens gibt es damit eine Brechung, und zweitens macht es noch etwas fremder und ferner*' (Fassbinder, 1986, p.56). But its effect is not one of straightforward alienation of the viewer on social and formal levels. Fassbinder is well aware of the dialectical operations of Brechtian *Verfremdung*; the interruption of empathy is only forceful when there is something to interrupt, which is to say that *Fontane Effi Briest* produces as well as exposes the lure of narcissistic identification. It activates an alienating performance from the actors precisely by making them identify with their own image in order to interrupt their identification with the character (Fassbinder, 1986, p.56); their *Haltung* as they play before the mirror thus functions counter-narcissistically. As Fassbinder says of his *Chinesisches Roulette* (1976), the mirrors at once propagate the social rituals enacted before them and break them in a way which is intended to impress itself subliminally on the spectator and enable him/her to break with the ritual behaviours which sustain the bourgeois order (Fassbinder, 1986, p.89). This political appeal to the spectator's unconscious embodies the combination of Brechtian and Freudian alienations in Fassbinder's project for breaking narcissism.

In *Fontane Effi Briest* the mirror sponsors illusion in order to cut it short – at once by styling Hanna Schygulla as Effi into such an irresistibly iconic body-image, and by allowing the eye to be tricked into entering the space through the looking-glass, before being disillusioned. The two-dimensional space of the mirror links up with that of photographs or of the written page which also punctuate the film, and the characteristic white-outs which erase the material dimensions of the filmic world. However attractive, the mirror, in this sense, is always marked out as a frame for negative space.

There is a subversive double-meaning lurking in Fassbinder's programme for a Brechtian cinema (Jansen and Schütte, 1992, p.92):

> *Ich bin dafür, daß der Zuschauer im Kino oder im Fernsehen die Möglichkeit hat, bei sich selber über die Figuren Gefühle und Dinge zu aktivieren, aber trotzdem in der Struktur der Sache selber die Möglichkeit zur Reflexion gegeben ist, also daß die Inszenierung so ist, daß sie einen Abstand und darüber eine Reflexion möglich macht.*

The '*Möglichkeit zur Reflexion*' is always likely to be a hybrid, dialectical combination of critical reflection on systems of construction and specular reflection in alluringly constructed images. *Fontane Effi Briest* remains a cinematic show, the mirror the prime device for showing, but one which is angled to show the act of showing. It acts, in other words, in accordance with the first principle of the Brechtian *Gestus*: '*Zeigen, daß gezeigt wird*. For Brecht's *Gestus*, we can read Fassbinder's *Einstellung* (Jansen and Schütte, 1992, p.113) or *Haltung* here, the at once technical and moral-political setting and posture of his filmmaking. In particular in the case of literary adaptation this means, as he notes in the case of *Querelle* (1982), '*die eindeutige Haltung des Fragens*' (Fassbinder, 1984, p.116), an interrogative stance rather than a complementary mirroring of the text. And what it demands of the viewer, in the case of *Fontane Effi Briest*, is, according to Fassbinder (1986, p.55), a form of critical reading:

> *Es ist der Versuch, einen Film ganz klar für den Kopf zu machen, also einen Film, in dem man nicht aufhört zu denken, sondern anfängt zu denken, und wie man beim Lesen Buchstaben und Sätze erst durch die Phantasie zu einer Handlung macht, so sollte es auch in diesem Film passieren. Also jeder sollte die Möglichkeit und die Freiheit haben, diesen Film zu seinem eigenen zu machen, wenn er ihn sieht; und das funktioniert meiner Ansicht nach nur über die dreifache Verfremdung, über die Distanz, die da stattfindet.*

The techniques of Fassbinder's '*dreifache Distanz*' (mirrorings, white-outs, and dispassionate performance) thus allow *Fontane Effi Briest* to work through a dialectic which can be called counter-narcissistic. They enable the viewer to identify with the film, to appropriate it as his/her own fantasy, and yet only through the alienating effect of rolling the narcissistic allure of film back into the more distanced effects of the written text. Fassbinder (1984, p.13) claims in his review of the film-making of his great model, Douglas Sirk, that the intensive experience of the spectator is effected in Sirk's films by '*Montage und Musik*' rather than identification. In Fassbinder's own aesthetic the mounting of cinematic space into relays of mirrors produces a particular form of montage, at once breaking identification and reconstructing it in a more carefully articulated form. His claim (1986, p.61) that the imagery of *Fontane Effi Briest* might function as '*Schwarzfilm*', a visual absence onto which the spectator may project his/her own film of the script, is excessive. But the dismantling and remounting which he practises on its visuals does achieve the sort of structural activation of the

124

spectator/consumer as critical reader which Adorno advocated for film through the use of montage. Alongside the images of text in the film, the visual montage shifts things, in Adorno's terms, into a ' *schrifthafte Konstellation*' (Adorno, 1967, p.84). It thereby represents a possibility for disrupting the seductive appeal of the filmic mirror and its full display of image, turning it into the blanker, more testing look of the written page, and so countering the narcissistic economy of the culture industry.

3 Wim Wenders: *Im Lauf der Zeit*

Im Lauf der Zeit is no less self-reflexive than Fassbinder's film. It is a film about film and, in every sense, its apparatus: its aesthetic conventions, its history, its fantasies, its commerce, and its equipment. As different as the two films are in their subject and scope, *Im Lauf der Zeit* shares with *Fontane Effi Briest* a counter-narcissistic *Einstellung*. This is marked partly by a similar strategic return to monochrome, adopting a screen aesthetic which corresponds to the black and white of the written page and of the photograph (as thematised in newspaper printing), and of early cinema (as represented, *inter alia,* by Fritz Lang as a sort of foster-father presence). Wenders, too, plays out his own repertoire of auteurist stylisations and signatures, culminating in the device of signing off with the WW monogram, putting his name in broken lights on the Weisse Wand cinema at the end of the film. The signature represents an emblematic advertisement for the new wave director, finding ways of asserting his identity through and in spite of the dysfunctional apparatus of the film industry.

Im Lauf der Zeit follows a key model of counter-narcissistic adventure: the road-movie as a journey through alienation. It operates a particular cinematic version of Stendhal's famous conceit of the realist text as a mirror, recording what passes as it travels down an open road. Wenders's motorised vehicle is a much more sophisticated model, a relay of reflective screens, front- and rearview windows, projecting multiple reflections, inner and outer, forward and backward. Above all, this complex post-realist mirror-machine, tracking along the border-country between the two Germanies, is always also angled at the

125

alienated roadster and his passenger. The buddies-in-alienation convention of the road-movie allows for a particular form of counter-narcissism, shared between men of the road. But the itinerant mirror-machine which is Wenders's film is no more prepared to mount an intact space for the counter-narcissists than it is to be the vehicle for an intact, mimetic continuity in its representation of the world.

As with Fontane–Fassbinder, the author's relation both to his protagonist and to the world of his film (here, in large part a film-world) is one of distinct ambivalence, as is, in its turn, the relation which the film allows the viewer. The motor of the film-journey is, not least, a desire for identification; the author–director, the protagonists, and the viewer are all in search of a reflection of their own identity in that of their fellow-travellers and in the experiences of their travels. But the network of potential identification which is constructed through the film is always interrupted by the effects of alienation. As in *Fontane Effi Briest*, the insistent on-screen presence of mirrors, the foregrounding of the apparatus of reflection, functions as a mark of estrangement in identification: an alienation effect.

The on-screen relationship between the driver, the cineastic projection engineer Bruno, and his passenger, Robert, models the difficulty of any counter-narcissistic relationship between *auteur* and film-viewer via the mirroring apparatus of the film. Timothy Corrigan (1981–2) has discussed the significance, for patterns of desire in the film, of the scene where Bruno and Robert act out their shadow-play behind the cinema-screen to the delight of the children waiting for the dysfunctional cinema machinery to be mended. This spectacle, providing a sort of revival of the silent, pantomimic origins of the cinema, is also an opportunity for a counter-narcissistic entertainment to supersede the more advanced productions of the film industry. The two players are, as it were, performing on a mirror-stage through specular projections of themselves. But this collusion is estranged by resistance to being mirrored by and with the other. The counter-narcissistic adventure is turned back into alienation when the two men aggressively discuss the performance afterwards. Standing in front of the whitewashed windows of an old van, they are framed by a sort of blanked-out mirror-image of the film's most recurrent shot which features the two men in the cab seen from the front through the reflective surface of the windscreen. The breakdown of the reciprocal relation (the one watching the other watching him) is thus cast through a sort of negative reflection of a shared mirror-space.

The immobile old van without mirrors represents the breakdown which shadows the time-travels of the men in the mirror-machine. It is a reflection of the blank screen in the dysfunctional cinema, briefly brought to life as a mirror for an alternative form of performance. The two forms of mirror-machine, truck and cinema, have a reflexive relationship in this road-movie, as Corrigan (1981–2, p.103) points out when he notes how insistently the film puts the projection booth and the auditorium face-to-face with the oncoming image of the men in the cab. This frontal shot as it were reflects back on the kings of the road, setting the film into a persistent reverse angle which shows the journey only as reflections in the glass and windows of the cab and highlights instead the viewers who direct it.

This strategy of mirroring the film back onto the protagonists and the apparatus which drives it is mirrored in its turn in the scene where the projectionist in one of the cinemas is found by Bruno masturbating in the projection booth. The scene shows a sort of narcissistic short-circuit in the cinematic machine. It is traced by Bruno from a curious blank spot at the centre of the image in the porn film being screened in the cinema. The blank operates as a sign of dysfunction in a machine which, particularly in the case of pornographic voyeurism, works by the narcissistic projection of the viewer into the scene on screen. This mirroring apparatus is made to dysfunction precisely by the insertion into the projector of a small mirror-device which allows the projectionist to project the film onto the back wall of the booth so that he can go through the motions of the sex-act as an imitative, narcissistic spectacle. The blank spot, mirrored out of the mirror-image on the cinema screen, thus connects with the other blankings we have seen of cinema screen and windscreen. This can be seen as a parody of counter-narcissism, reflecting the cinematic mirror-image back for auto-erotic pleasure, rather than a critically alienating appropriation. When Bruno cuts together his own film out of footage from the porn movie and then projects it in an interminable loop of sex and violence, he is as it were parodying that parody. He, too, is mirroring the film for a private showing, but by his strategic cutting and montage, he produces a mirroring only of the radical alienation which drives the film industry through the dominant discourses which feature on his film's soundtrack: '*Härte, Action, Sinnlichkeit*'.

While Bruno's film acts as a sort of emblematic *mise-en-abîme* (the film-within-the-film as a mirroring device which subverts the spectacle which frames it), it offers no real possibility for alternative viewing. It is part, however, of the machinery of more constructive appropriation of the film apparatus which Wenders activates in *Im Lauf der Zeit*. The counter-narcissistic strategies of the film cumulatively construct an alternative framework for the production of more careful identifications through the dismantling and remounting of the cinematic mirror-machine.

4 Margarethe von Trotta: *Die bleierne Zeit*

Die bleierne Zeit may be seen as a counterpart to *Im Lauf der Zeit*. Both films state their concern with time and the times, but here the story of prodigal sons makes way for that of prodigal daughters. At first sight von Trotta seems to be less concerned here to produce counter-narcissistic stylisations than either Fontane or Wenders. But the political engagement and documentary basis of *Die bleierne Zeit* should not be mistaken for naive realism. As we shall see, von Trotta adopts the two most coventional devices for the production of realism (the mimetic mirror and the window on the world) and proceeds to alienate their effects and thereby estrange the viewer's desire for a narcissistic capture of the filmic world.

The film is insistently structured. This can be seen not least in its alternations between interiors and exteriors. In the screenplay ' *Außen*' and '*Innen*' assume a significance beyond their role as conventional cinematographic markers. 'Outside' and 'inside' are bound up in a dialectic, a complex and sliding opposition, which corresponds to von

128

Trotta's attempt to mediate (1981, pp.78–9) between the political and the personal as represented respectively by her first and second films:

> *Mit diesem Film [...] versuche ich eine Synthese zwischen meinem ersten und zweiten Film.* Das zweite Erwachen der Christa Klages *war eine Bestandsaufnahme der äußeren Befindlichkeiten in der Bundesrepublik. Der zweite Film,* Schwestern oder Die Balance des Glücks, *konzentrierte sich auf Innenleben, auf Emotionen und Gefühle, die natürlich auch abhängig sind von dem, was wir in unserer Gesellschaft vorfinden.* Die bleierne Zeit *wird beide Ebenen haben, nach innen und außen blicken.*

The look of von Trotta's film is thus split between inner and outer views. This bifocal perspective is constructed into the film by the use of walls and windows, thematised in imprisonments both of a systematic social kind and of a personal subjective kind. As in Fassbinder's film, social space is always under surveillance here, and it irresistibly infringes any sort of intimacy of personal space. Here, narcissism represents a certain opportunity for finding community of identity between sisters, a sort of utopian feminist dyad posed within and against a patriarchal system. Von Trotta arrogates for her sisters what is conventionally, as I have argued elsewhere (Webber, 1996), the masculine prerogative of the *Doppelgänger.* But the confusion of self and other as *alter ego* proves as problematic for the female subject here as for the male subject in the texts and films of the *Doppelgänger* tradition.

This is the sort of double identity which is played out as a spectacle in a childhood scene from the earlier film, *Schwestern oder Die Balance des Glücks,* when the two sisters make themselves up in front of a dressing-table mirror, and their laughing faces are projected in a gallery of mirror-images. This flashback, played without its natural soundtrack, appeals to a narcissistic fantasy of being one with the other as pure image, prior to the separations organised by language. The girls' mouths only laugh in a mute echo, and they exchange this key feature of their body-image by imprinting lipstick kisses on each other's cheeks.

The scene corresponds to the model of the Lacanian Mirror Stage as the primal scenario of the order of body images and identifications which Lacan calls the Imaginary. But just as, in Lacanian theory, the infant's narcissistic capture of its mirror-image is only a surface for a more troubled sense of identity, so this scene troubles the desire of the viewer to identify with the players. The mute, multiple mirror-space is experienced as much as one of hermetic constraint as of primal unity. And the lipstick, as a marker of the cosmetic fashioning which is required of the female body-image in patriarchal society, also imprints the scene with signs of Lacan's master order, the order of social organisation which he calls the Symbolic. In this sense, the flashback scene is a rehearsal for the conflict between the sisters' narcissistic confluence and the demands of social relations (women made up to play gender roles dictated by male voices and interests) which is enacted to catastrophic effect in the adult story of the film.

In the more expressly political context of its sister-film, *Die bleierne Zeit*, narcissistic community between sisters is also ultimately cast into alienated forms. Here, too, the Mirror Stage proves to be a model for estrangement of the self in its internal and external relations. The childhood mirror-scene of *Schwestern* is, as it were, projected into the extraordinary jail-scene of *Die bleierne Zeit*, which at the same time mirrors the famous merging of facial identities in Bergman's *Persona*. It also serves to redouble many of the reflexive images, scenes, and sequences which can be seen to characterise *Die bleierne Zeit* as a whole. The scene mediates the narcissistic fantasy of identity with the sister through the total apparatus of imprisonment and surveillance. A window-wall – a conflation, that is, of those two structural *leitmotifs* – is made to serve as a type of two-way mirror. It is a scene which distorts and fragments speech and vision through an all-seeing and all-hearing system, and produces a powerful image of grotesque alienation: an image of non-identity which is as much political as it is personal.

It is worth considering in detail the highly complex *Einstellung* of this counter-narcissistic scene. The scene is set up by a sequence of telling reflexive effects. First Juliane receives and reads a letter from Marianne, featuring – in conventional cinematic style, but with a twist here – the voice-over of Marianne reading out Juliane's reading of the letter. At the same time the scene is mediated by a play of mirrors worthy of *Fontane*

Effi Briest, as the camera lures the viewer unawares into the reflected space of a first mirror, only to project the reading in a second, facing mirror. As we see Juliane reading with Marianne's voice, face-on in the mirror, so the scenario of confusion for voice and image in the prison is previewed.

The intermediary scene – Juliane approaching the prison on a bus – is no less marked out as scene-setting, not only in the conventional sense of establishing the scene to come by viewing it from outside, but also prefiguring its *Einstellung* through a complex set of alienating effects. As Juliane's view tracks along the prison wall and up to the watch-tower which stands as the sign of a panoptical system of control, the window of the bus is reflected into view. Rather than working transparently, the window reflects an image of the viewer, and as window and wall are superimposed so Juliane is obliquely projected into a sort of window-wall. She is outside the system of imprisonment and correction, yet also projected into it.

It might be tempting to scrutinise the sequence filmed through the mirror-window of the bus for reflections of the filming apparatus as well as of the protagonist. This subtle indication of estrangement in the scene's mimetic function is echoed in another telling function of the vehicle which is apparently only there to transport the story-line to the penitentiary. As the function of the image is challenged so is that of sound. The mechanical apparatus of the bus (illuminated sign and microphone) produces the most routine of signalling effects, but here it functions in a Brechtian manner, serving to expose a more general apparatus of social control. The voice which names the scene is denaturalised into a sort of voice-over effect through its mediation by machinery, specifically the sort of microphone which will provide the apparatus for the transmission of speech in the prison visiting room.

The voice-overs of the two establishing scenes establish, then, a disjunction between present experience and speech. The prison scene itself takes this up through Juliane's voice-over narrative as the camera follows her in. The dramatic presence of the scene, and thus its appeal to immediate identification, is refracted, in Brechtian style, into a historicising narrative: a reconstruction of events. Its controlled, epic style is in marked contrast to the use of speech in the scene, but this too is estranged, passing either via a third person or the apparatus for communication. The scene thus functions according to a Brechtian *Trennung der Elemente*, whereby its sound-track is interrupted and thus dissociated from the visual field.

As in the scene from *Schwestern*, the encounter here is set up in theatrical fashion as a kind of mirror-stage, with the sisters and their attendants arranged symmetrically on either side of the glass partition. This imitation of a mirror is then developed through a complex series of reflexive effects, as the sisters' movements are coordinated, the images of their faces merge and split, match and mismatch. The turning towards and away from each other of the physical faces and their reflections enacts a visual drama cast between a counter-narcissistic relation (the sisters identifying in spite of the apparatus) and alienation (such as when they appear to be turning towards each other like mirror-images, but it is only their mirror-images which are doing so as they separately respond to their separation by the warders).

The realist conventions of the film, its continuity editing of sound and image, seem to break down in this scene. The monstrous distortion it produces creates a cinematic mirror-image which can only profoundly estrange the viewer's desire for identification. As Marianne is lead away, the final communication is an alienated version of the shot-reverse-shot convention, apparently allowing both points of view to share the same frame. In fact the apparent merger is misdirected and disconnected by its mediation through the mirroring partition. It ends in Juliane's solitary and virtual image in the glass wall.

Von Trotta's version of the mirror-stage is, then, a complex and traumatic one. The dramatisation of merging and splitting in this scene, the sisters' final one together, marks the ultimate subjection of counter-narcissistic revolt to the dominant system of a narcissistic culture. Like *Im Lauf der Zeit, Die bleierne Zeit* is clear-sighted about the power of that culture and the difficulties involved in any forms of resistance to it. The film eschews heroicisation of the sisters as resistance fighters, but it ultimately registers a certain, albeit tentative, movement towards new possibilities for identification. The closing scene, and the communication it promises, sets up a model for retelling experience which will not simply combat first-order narcissism with second-order narcissism, but will always be as vigilant as possible in testing the ground of a projected identity in which we might participate.

5 Edgar Reitz: *Heimat*

At first sight, Edgar Reitz's monumental chronicle of life in a Hunsrück village, *Heimat,* would seem to have little to do with the alienations of identity and ideology in von Trotta's film. However, here too there is strategic distortion at work in the cinematic mirror. If I suggested that the *Heimatfilm* of the 1950s and 1960s created a particularly crude mirror for the culture of narcissism, then *Heimat* remirrors that model to produce more complex reflections on and of the German homeland. The film is conceived as a reaction to what Reitz sees as the cultural imperialism of America and its film industry which engages in expropriating the images and stories of Germany's history. His strategic reappropriation of the means of its reproduction is not, however, without its problems; problems of sentimentality and of selective vision. Gertrud Koch (1985, p.13) has argued, for instance, that 'in order to tell the myth of *Heimat,* the trauma of Auschwitz had to be bracketed from German history'. In this sense, and through the focal role of the autobiographical hero, the film has its own share in narcissism. If this is inevitable in the depiction of *Heimat,* as the place which reflects your own primal experience, it is also bound to be a site of estrangement, of loss of innocence, not least in the case of Germany. For Reitz, *Heimat* is never readily accessible, but always subject to what he views as the dialectical operation of Romanticism. It can be rendered present, in other words, only through degrees of absence.

The film operates dialectically on viewers, especially German ones, who look to it for a mirror of their own experience. It activates the narcissistic lure of what Baudrillard has called the 'retro-scenario' (Elsaesser, 1989, p.254), but the nostalgia it offers is always qualified by difference. The film *Heimat* is never a site for direct identifications; it always puts the viewer into the role of ethnographic tourist, as you re-experience through this other *Heimat* your relationship to your own, which you in a sense possess, but of which you are always substantially dispossessed. This is *Heimat* the theme-park, as indeed it is on the way to becoming by the end of Reitz's film, as its features are commodified, its furniture odorised with rustic sprays to give it the authentic scent of the *Heimat* of 1865 and sold off to homes in the city.

This processing, reproduction, and displacement of *Heimat* reflects upon Reitz's own enterprise. He started with a scripted ' *Filmroman*', but let it be part rewritten through improvisation and peopled in part by genuine Hunsrück character-actors. The epic work of construction saw history, not least Reitz's biographical history, displaced into what he recognises as a cooperative ' *Fiktion*' (Reitz and Steinbach, 1984, p.5). What the film constructs is a fantasy mirror of a *Heimat* which hordes of displaced TV tourists scoured the Hunsrück to find and see themselves in.

Reitz is well aware of the contradictions within his enterprise. Indeed the title sequence can be read as emblematic of the tensions within the work. The title *Heimat* is projected out of some prehistoric stone, set on an archetypal German heath which is anachronistically inscribed with the trademark of the *Wirtschaftswunder*: 'Made in Germany'. The glossy cinematic letters of light which form the second title are also reflective, mirroring the clouds which race over them. The opening of the chronicle thus moves from the epic lettering of apparently immutable mythical identities to more glamorous and transitory projections representing a fast-forward view of history. The mirroring in the letters of *Heimat* projected out of the memorial stone sets up a complex vehicle for identification: a projection at once of private and national narcissism and mourning for viewers who might see themselves in the mirror of this film and find that they are inscribed as made in Germany. It is an emblem of the film's fundamental *Gestus*, following the Brechtian model of *Zeigen, daß gezeigt wird*, where to show means to construct an image for showing. This construction is marked throughout by the staging of scenes for photographic records, and the showing of these by the chronicler, Glasisch, as a prelude to the film-show at the beginning of each episode. The exposure of the archaic technologies of representation and communication – camera and wireless – acts, according to Reitz (Reitz, 1993, p.19), as a *Verfremdungseffekt*. They

134

show that what is mourned in the loss of *Heimat* is not simply a primal or natural thing, but a construction; a construction which Reitz's film self-consciously reconstructs. Like Syberberg's filmic version of Hitler, this is a film made in and of Germany. It represents a self-reflexive questioning of the making and making up of the home-movie of *Heimat.* Its narcissism is, in other words, angled through techniques of counter-narcissism.

The question remains whether these latter function as a sufficient corrective to the seduction of the mirror, or whether critics like Koch are right in suggesting that the film's specularity merely serves to sustain an ideology of sanitisation. While Reitz's film cannot be said uncritically to present a regressive Mirror Stage to the German viewer, it is certainly arguable whether it does enough to challenge the power exerted by the cultural Imaginary in the form of clean and intact images of communal life.

The use of mirrorings, both actual and metaphorical, in the film illustrates at least a potential for challenging the dominance of the narcissistic *Einstellung* by means of a more self-critical *Gestus.* The ambivalent emblem of the opening titles can be traced through the reflexive structures and mirror-imagery of the film. The film is structured through leitmotifs, scenes which mirror earlier scenes. These certainly construct forms of retro-scenario within the film's own memory, mirror it back on itself, but they also typically mark the loss of, and alienation from, earlier scenes.

In a number of cases these structural reflections are mediated by mirrors. In an early scene, Pauline's reflection is caught in the show-case mirror of the jeweller's shop, as she is showered by shattered glass in anticipation of the *Kristallnacht.* The splinter in her finger, which might have festered, is removed as her hand is taken in a marriage which will prosper at the expense of Jews. It is an apparently superficial trauma, one which is, though, only apparently healed. It returns to her as a sort of hysterical symptom when she is once more mirrored in the window later in the film with the SA parading behind her. The profound trauma of the holocaust is thus only subtly reflected into the world of *Heimat.* This points up fractures in its narcissistic mirror and the identities which

135

it projects, but fractures which the narcissistically inclined viewer might succeed in overlooking.

The film's opening emblem is mirrored back in the final episode when the prodigal son sees his image reflected in the polished tomb-stone of his grand-parents' grave. And this morbid mirror-image becomes, in its turn, the model for a whole series of scenes of alienated self-reflection for the expatriot Hermann in the sequel, *Die zweite Heimat*. Hermann, the self-exiled counter-narcissist, always remains partly captivated by the primal narcissism of the Heimat he has left behind him and the constitutional *Heimweh* which it produces.

Reitz had originally planned a dialectical structure for *Heimat*, starting out from a position of loss with the death of the matriarch Maria, and alternating between present-day sequences and flash-back. Even without this framework of alienation, however, the film is no straightforward hymn to a lost place and time. The framework is perhaps effaced, but it is always also present in more oblique forms, not least in what Reitz calls, after Brecht, the *Gestus* of the characters: the element of show, which always marks their naturalness as unnatural, ritualised and cultivated (1984, p.148). *Heimat*, in other words, performs or reproduces itself through what Reitz calls ' *die Dialektsprache als Sprachtheater*' (1984, p.148). What might appear to be the regressive Mirror Stage of *Heimat* is thus intended to be a more self-conscious mirror-stage, a theatre for self-representation, always aware of its own performance.

Reitz made his 'Made in Germany' film in order to counter colonisation by the extrinsic culture of Hollywood and what he calls ' *der tiefste Verlust, der Verlust der eigenen Sprache*' (1984, p.142). But the more intrinsic loss of identity with and in your own language, both verbal and visual, is also the story of his film, as are the dangers involved in trying to re-appropriate it. Indeed, this is the story of all four films considered here. They all recognise the need to dismantle false identities and to construct a more authentic sense of selfhood, and thereby to answer the primal demand of identification in the viewer. But any such identity must always be subjected to interrogation, in order to expose, through *Verfremdung*, any narcissistic sleights, and thus to encourage the viewer to resist the lure of too ready or familiar forms of identification. Albeit with varying degrees of success, these 'new German' films can be said to project a more honest reflection of German identities and of the alienating distortions which are inherent in the ideological act of identifying a viable *Heimat* for yourself.

Bibliography

Adorno T W, *Ohne Leitbild: Parva Aesthetica* (Frankfurt am Main, Suhrkamp, 1967)

Corrigan T, 'Wenders's *Kings of the Road:* The voyage from desire to language' in: *New German Critique* (24–25, Fall/Winter 1981–2, pp.94–107, 1981–2)

Elsaesser T, *New German Cinema: A history.* (Basingstoke, Macmillan, 1989)

Fassbinder R W, edited by Töteberg M, *Filme befreien den Kopf: Essays und Arbeitsnotizen* (Frankfurt am Main, Fischer, 1984)

————. edited by Töteberg M, *Die Anarchie der Phantasie: Gespräche und Interviews.* (Frankfurt am Main, Fischer, 1986)

Fontane T, *Effi Briest* (Munich, Goldmann, 1984)

Jansen P W und W Schütte (eds) *Rainer Werner Fassbinder* (Frankfurt am Main, Fischer, 1992)

Koch G, 'How much naiveté can we afford? The New *Heimat* feeling' in: *New German Critique* (36, Fall 1985, pp.13–16, 1985)

Lacan J, *Ecrits: A selection* (London, Tavistock, 1977)

Mitscherlich A und M, *Die Unfähigkeit zu trauern* (Munich, Piper, 1977)

Reitz E und P Steinbach, *Heimat: Eine deutsche Chronik* (Frankfurt am Main, Verlag der Autoren, 1984)

Reitz E, *Liebe zum Kino* (Cologne, Köln 78, 1984)

————. edited by Töteberg M, *Drehort Heimat: Arbeitsnotizen und Zukunftsentwürfe* (Frankfurt am Main, Verlag der Autoren, 1993)

Trotta M von, ed. Weber H J, *Die bleierne Zeit: Ein Film von Margarethe von Trotta* (Frankfurt am Main, Fischer, 1981)

Webber A J, *The 'Doppelgänger': Double visions in German literature.* (Oxford, Clarendon Press, 1996)